A FARMER'S LAD

MEMOIRS OF A RURAL SOLICITOR

Geoff Tomlinson

Published by Zaccmedia
www.zaccmedia.com
info@zaccmedia.com

Published March 2014

ISBN: 978-1-909824-28-7

British Library Cataloguing-in-Publication Data
A catalogue record for this book is available from the British Library

Illustrations by Dan Clement
Cover photography by Paul Stanier, Zaccmedia

CONTENTS

PREFACE

Why write my memoirs? Is that not a little self-indulgent and is it not slightly arrogant even to imagine that anyone might have the slightest desire to read them?

There are several answers to that question. 'You should write a book about that some day' has been said to me a number of times in the course of my career in the law, usually just after a particularly interesting or amusing incident has occurred, or perhaps when I have been recounting the tale later.

I first got the idea when I came across a book with the splendid title of *The Doings of a Country Solicitor*, the autobiography of Alexander Pearson, a solicitor who practised in Kirkby Lonsdale in Westmorland for over 50 years from 1934. He lived and practised law in an era hugely different from the one I have known and his account gives a fascinating insight into the life of a rural solicitor in the pre-war years in particular. However, many of the principles which he espoused, such as the importance of getting to know and understand your clients and the fundamental principle of integrity, are of course timeless. It does no harm at all to remind ourselves of such things as we move further into the 21st century.

What really brought the idea into focus was the decision by the partners in my firm to allow me to reduce my working week to three days with effect from 1st October 2011, in anticipation of my full retirement in March 2014, just after my sixtieth birthday.

At a time like that you do tend to think about such things. My conclusion was 'Why not?' So I had to decide what kind of book it should be and what I would actually say in it. I knew immediately that I didn't want it to be self-indulgent (the modern phrase is 'vanity publishing') and that it should certainly not become some kind of rant. I do have my views on certain issues, but if they have emerged during the course of what I have written I hope that I have managed to be gracious – honestly! I also hope that I have been frank about my own shortcomings.

In the preface to the first edition of his book, written in May 1947, Alexander Pearson said:

'In the month of April 1945, while lying in a Manchester Nursing Home, after an operation, in order to help pass the time, I sent to the stationers for some exercise books and wrote in them such tales about some of my ancestors and accounts of my personal doings as I thought might be of interest to members of my family. "Do tell me what you are writing about," said the sister in charge of my quarters, as she came in to see me one evening, so I handed her all my manuscript in order that she might see for herself. She returned it the next morning when making her rounds, and asked me as a personal favour to go on with and finish my story, saying that she had read what I had written already with such very great interest and pleasure and that in the same way she had enjoyed it, so would others beside my relations and she felt sure that my memoirs, if published, would be

welcomed by the general public, especially by those who were invalids, or were thankful for anything readable which might give them amusement and interest and help them forget their troubles.'

When I read that, it occurred to me that even if only a few people were sufficiently interested (or bored or incapacitated) to read my story, there might just be a chance of raising some money for a good cause. That would have to be one connected with farming. RABI (the Royal Agricultural Benevolent Institution) was the obvious choice and I am very grateful to Georgina Lamb and her colleagues at RABI for agreeing to the proposition which I put to her when we met at Westmorland Show in 2012.

We agreed that I would pay for (or at least underwrite) the publication and printing of the initial run of this book, and that RABI would promote it and keep all the sale proceeds. So come on, folks, buy an extra copy or two for your friends (or maybe for your enemies if you don't think much of it!).

I do hope that you enjoy reading about my journey through life and my professional career and, like Alexander Pearson before me, that it will give you 'amusement and interest' and help you forget your troubles, if only for a little while.

Chapter One

A FARMER'S LAD

My Roots and Upbringing

I was born on 14th March 1954 in a council house in Broughton, near Preston, Lancashire, the third child of Ralph Gardner Tomlinson (1924–2012) and Dorothy (Dot) Tomlinson (1924–2003). I was christened Geoffrey Ralph, but I have never liked being called Geoffrey (so if you want to annoy me, you now know how) and have always preferred to be known as Geoff. At that time, dad was working for his father, John (Jack) Tomlinson, at Newsham Lodge, Woodplumpton, the family farm in the next village, little more than a mile away. Mum was also from a farming family, the middle one of the three daughters of Arthur and Agnes Porter of Lane Ends Farm, Preesall, near Poulton le Fylde, also in Lancashire. I never knew my grandfather Arthur, because he died when I was two, but I wish I had because mum told me that he was a kind and gentle man. I have only ever seen a couple of photographs of him, but I'm pleased to say that I now have one of them.

My grandmother Agnes was born just over the border in

Above left: Yes, I did have blonde curls at one time in my life – as a toddler!

Above right: When I was aged five or six: note the judicious use of Brylcreem.

Yorkshire (her parents were the licensees of the Punchbowl Inn at Low Bentham) but she had the good sense to move to Lancashire as a young woman and she stayed here for the rest of her life.

Dad's family had been farmers for generations. His dad originated from Hillock Farm, Warton, near Preston, but he farmed at Balderstone Farm, Woodplumpton; Crown Lane Farm near Catforth; and Church Farm, Singleton (for a couple of years during World War Two), before he bought Newsham Lodge in 1943. At 45 acres it would have been an average size for a farm in the area at that time, but it would be very small by modern standards.

The family had kept pigs, sheep, hens and cows at Newsham Lodge, but by the time I was old enough to remember, dad had just about turned it into an exclusively dairy enterprise, although he did actually keep hens for a few more years after that. In 1956 my dad's parents retired to a bungalow, 'Longacre', which they had had built on the lane which led into the farm. Grandad was only 56, which was a very young age at which to retire in those days, but I got the impression that he had never been too keen on work even before that. When he was in charge he had been more of a gentleman farmer. My dad and his younger brother Alan were working at home then and in addition to them I understand that the farm always had a couple of other workers. Grandad had enjoyed going to the races, and I gather that he was also fond of his whisky. Mum used to tell me that he had had a good time during the war, socialising with his mates in Blackpool. He apparently made quite a bit of money selling farm produce on the black market, including to one of his co-conspirators who owned a hearse, in which he used to drive to the farm on a regular basis, hiding the eggs, ham and bacon and other produce beneath the rear compartment.

My parents' courting years were also during the war. In those days, dances in village halls played a large part in their social life. Dad used to travel to dance halls in the farm's van and he would get round the fact that petrol was rationed by ensuring that he always had a tray of eggs in the back. So, if he was stopped at night by a village bobby when on such an outing, he could always claim that he was on the way to deliver some eggs! I'm not sure how convincing that story will have been, but I suspect that the way dad and farming lads like him stayed out of trouble had more to do with the village policemen never being without an egg or two for their breakfasts, and probably the odd rasher of home-cured bacon as well. Mum used to say that the menfolk on the farm would often go out at night to kill a pig – when I was little I remember the six-inch nails which were still in the exposed beams in the attic rooms of the farmhouse, nails on which numerous hams had been hung during those war years.

I struggle to remember my grandad doing a day's work, although for a few years after he retired he would look after the farm for a week in the summer so my parents could take my older sisters Jen and Kath and myself on holiday. We went to Butlins at Skegness (which seemed very exotic) and to the Isle of Man, but by the time I was about 15 or 16 I was looking after the farm so my parents could go away for a week. I did all the milking and all the other work myself. My sister Julie, born in 1963, and therefore nine years younger than me, also undertook the farm work for a year or two later on, but by then I had already left home.

It's no more than a theory on my part, but a revealing fact which came to my attention in 1974 may possibly help to explain the attitude and behaviour of my grandad. It was my grandparents' Golden Wedding Anniversary that summer and a family party was held at the farm. At one point we all gathered in the front garden for a photograph. I think it was in June, but in any event I was home from university. On 31st October of that year dad celebrated his fiftieth birthday. Oops! Until then I had no idea that my grandparents had had to get married in 1924, when he was 24 and she was 18. Fancy that!

They did have a honeymoon, in Derbyshire, in fact. They were sheltering under a tree during a storm when they met a local farmer's son, whose name also turned out to be Tomlinson. They became friends with Allan Tomlinson and his family, and not only did that friendship last for the rest of their lives, but my parents also maintained a long friendship with Allan's son Allan and his wife Lucy. Isn't it strange how such things can come about?

One thing about my grandad which I did come to appreciate in later years was that his everyday speech included many dialect words. For example, when referring to a female he would always say 'oo' rather than 'she', as in *'Oo was in the garden.'* He also had his own version of a saying which I suspect is used in many parts of the country, or at least in those parts in which hills are in view. Eastwards from Newsham Lodge there was a good view of the hills on a clear day, and grandad used to say (in dialect), *'If tha con see th'ills it's banna rain, and if tha cawnt it's rainin.'* If you don't understand that, ask a 'Lanky' to translate!

The sad thing about grandad was that he didn't really have any interests outside farming, so it seemed to me that after he retired he just sat in the chair and waited to die, which happened when he was 82.

My dad didn't make the same mistake. By his early sixties he had retired and taken up Crown Green bowling with a vengeance! He was a good player and enjoyed playing competitive bowls for twenty years or more, until he became too frail to continue. At one stage he was playing for three different teams each week, something which didn't always go down too well with mum. He also maintained his interest in farming after he retired, still attending livestock auctions and farm sales for a good number of years. Into his eighties he was an active member of Goosnargh Farmers' Club (one of many such clubs at which I have been a guest speaker over the years).

My grandma Tomlinson was a totally different character from her husband. She also hailed from a farming family in the Fylde and was born Ellen Gardner (hence dad's middle name), but she was known as Nelly. She was a lively character and had a real sense of fun, but on the other hand mum used to say that when she and dad were newly married Nelly was really quite cruel to her. For example, she insisted on mum going back to work in the house within twenty-four hours of the birth of her first child, when mum wasn't well enough and understandably wanted to spend more time with her new baby.

When grandad retired, my parents moved to Newsham Lodge, together with my two older sisters and myself (then aged two). Farming wasn't dad's first choice of career. He was an intelligent man. Having done very well academically, he was lined up to go to university when he left school in 1942 and he really wanted to become a vet, but then grandad had a nervous breakdown and dad had to stay at home to run the farm. By the time grandad recovered, dad had missed his chance of an alternative career, and the result was that he ended up milking cows for the next forty years. However, as I said at dad's funeral in 2012, if he resented that, he never said so and he did go on to make a very good job of being a farmer.

Dad never said much; in fact he never really discussed important things and the truth is that we weren't close as father and son. He kept his plans and his worries to himself, although occasionally he did allow things to get on top of him and he could become quite depressed. He also had a fairly bad temper; for example, he would explode and curse and swear if a cow wasn't doing what he wanted it to do. As a child, I also had a terrible temper and would blow my top and lash out with what was probably very little provocation. That did change, as I will explain in chapter two.

I'm sure my dad's own father didn't set him a very good example. My parents had grown up in an age of austerity, their formative years as teenagers occurring during World War Two. They were both pretty determined characters, if not stubborn, but mum particularly so. My three sisters and I grew up understanding that if things went against us there was no point complaining; you just had to get on with life. As I said at dad's funeral, the four of us all have different personalities, but in our own ways we all also have that same determination and stubborn streak and I'm sure that our upbringing has helped to make us all independent and self-reliant. As I also remarked at the funeral, though, the other side of that coin is that it has been known for each of us to be accused of being insensitive!

As a farmer, dad was quite forward-thinking and he was prepared to try new ideas. He had obviously realised early on that he would effectively have to run the farm on his own, so he set about turning it into a one-man operation. In the mid-sixties he installed a bulk milk tank and an early form of milk pipeline – an Alfa Laval RTS ('round the shed') system, for those who remember them – thereby turning an old shippon ('cowshed' to the uninitiated) into a form of milking parlour, all at pretty low cost. It was one of the first in our area. He built basic cow kennels from what was in effect a DIY kit (we later constructed more, thereby rendering redundant the remaining shippons). That meant that mucking-out could be done mechanically, with a scraper fitted onto the back of our 1955 Massey Harris Ferguson tractor ('Little Grey Fergy' to many people, although my sister Julie called ours 'Tiddley-Poo'), which we used to push the muck out through the double doors at the rear and then up a ramp into an open slurry lagoon which dad had had dug in what had once been an orchard. Believe me, that was much easier than mucking out four separate shippons of different sizes with a shovel and barrow. That had been my job for a number of years before that; I remember it being a particularly unpleasant one on cold winter mornings. It was warm enough inside the shippons, of course, but there were mornings when my hands would stick to the freezing-cold steel handles of the muck barrow (even through gloves, when I had them), and I remember having to break the ice on the midden at one end of the yard.

Muck-spreading was also a winter job. In those days, we had to load our small muck-spreader by hand, forkful by forkful, often standing in the midden with muck coming up near to the top of our wellies (at least our feet were warm then!). As with all such tasks there was a recommended technique. You had to create a wall of stiffer muck (usually with more straw in it) at the back of the spreader, so the sloppy stuff didn't run out before you had reached the field where the muck was to be spread. If the land

My sister Julie on Tiddley-Poo the tractor, 1966.

was soft you also had to remember not to try to set off spreading uphill, because Tiddley-Poo didn't have too much power and it was easy to get stuck if you didn't set off downhill. I did make that mistake once, and had to unload most of the muck by hand before I could get going. I never forgot again.

It was hard physical work, but one consolation was that when we had a break for dinner ('lunch' to southerners) mum would have a hot meal ready for us in the farmhouse kitchen, often a mountainous home-made meat-and-potato pie, which we would devour in no time.

Sometimes I would be working alongside dad when we were muck spreading, but friends from the village also would come to help if they were in need of extra pocket money. One of these was Graham Duncan, although for some reason he was always known as George. Various other lads from the village also worked for dad in those days, some on a regular part-time basis and others as casual workers, especially when we were still making hay (before we switched to silage). Making hay did require machinery, but dad had the minimum amount of machines necessary, and even some of these were ancient ones which had clearly been converted from earlier horse-drawn use, so that they could be pulled by a tractor. Dad used a contractor to bale the hay, another local farmer called David Cottam (his son Mark, who was then captain of the Colts team at Preston Grasshoppers, was a member of the party when I went on my first ever overseas rugby tour in 1978). When it was ready and the baling had been done, teams of us would follow with tractors and trailers to load the bales and then cart them back to the farm, where we stacked them in the very large barn within the main block of the farm buildings. That barn is now part of what I believe is a very luxurious house – how times change!

Back then, we actually had two tractors, but one of them was brought out only at hay-time and spent the rest of the year stored under an open-sided implement shed at the rear of the main farm buildings, along with our two four-wheeled trailers (devils to reverse!) and the rest of the hay-making machinery. That shed had a very large roof, with low eaves, and an occasional summer job was to re-tar its roof. The second tractor was a 'sit up and beg' Allis Chalmers, with orange paintwork and a petrol engine which made a distinctive 'pop, pop, pop' sound when it was running. I believe a lot of these were sent over from the USA during the war. I also remember playing on it as a kid. It would have been a collectors' item now and probably worth a few bob, but sadly it was sold for scrap when we no longer had any use for it – not one of my dad's better decisions as it turned out!

The same fate also befell an ex-US-Army truck (a 3-tonner I think) which for many years had lain abandoned in the field behind the implement shed. I never knew why it was there, but I guess it must have been used on the farm at some stage. All I knew was that it was a fun thing for a little boy to play in.

As well as casual labour from the village, hay-time also involved most of the family, and even grandad helped out for a year or two. That could be hard work, particularly when we had to row up cut grass by hand (using long-handled pitchforks), or worse still, to 'cock' it before forecast rain arrived. That process involved putting the hay into individual piles or 'cocks' (mini haystacks, I suppose); the idea being that most of the hay would be protected from the worst of the rain. This was grandad's favourite technique, but it was very labour-intensive and the rest of the family were not at all keen, especially since all of the cocks had to be dismantled by hand when the weather improved.

All of the family would gather for refreshments in the afternoon, at what we knew as 'bagin' time. That was the light meal we would always have before starting the evening milking (which of course still had to be done in hay-time), but in hay-time the treat was that we would have that meal in the field in which we were working. Mum would bring out a wicker basket filled with sandwiches, cakes and biscuits, and she would serve tea from a large brown enamel teapot. That is a particularly happy memory from my childhood, and as I think about those hot summer days I can almost smell the hay and feel the sun on my back. It wasn't quite *Darling Buds of May*, but it probably was the nearest we ever got to a family picnic.

Unloading the hay and stacking it in the barn was another difficult and tiring job, but I was young and fit and took it in my stride. We didn't have an elevator, so the bales (which could be quite heavy) all had to be thrown by hand, and as the stack grew higher that was done in relays. It was also hot work, especially if you were the one stacking the bales high up under the roof slates. We had to carry on working until the job was done (and then be up early the next morning for milking), and sometimes we wouldn't finish until very late at night, but then we would all troop into the farmhouse kitchen again, this time for mountains of ham and eggs and the like.

Looking back, I realise I grew up being used to hard work and that has stayed with me, although the nature of that work changed as it became a lot less physical. To this day, whatever else might be said about me, I don't think anyone could justifiably accuse me of being afraid of a hard day's work.

As you have probably gathered, food played a significant role in daily life on the farm, or at least it did before the work became more mechanised and therefore less labour-intensive. The normal pattern, which applied to me when I was not at school, was that we would get up at between six and six-thirty and get everything ready for milking (including bringing the cows in from the fields in summer, which was a great job on a sunny morning), at which point someone would bring out to the parlour a mug of tea and some toast. After milking was finished and all the equipment had been washed in the dairy and put away, we would have a full cooked breakfast. Depending on the time of year there would be a variety of other jobs to be done through the rest of the morning, such as mucking out (later scraping out) in winter, and before we started making silage the cows also had to be fed hay by hand during these cold months. That process, which we knew as 'fothering', involved carrying bales from the barn (penknife in pocket, ready to cut the strings) to each separate shippon and putting enough hay in front of each cow. This was done every day after breakfast and then again after tea, which meant you might have to rush through the process if you were going out for the evening. It could be an unpleasant job, especially if the hay was of poor quality, as that could make it very dusty. Other jobs to be done during the day would include muck-spreading in winter and fertiliser-spreading ('till-sowing' to us) in spring, and then there were always general farm maintenance jobs to be done whatever the time of year – but we were not very good at those and a lot of things tended to be mended with string. After the morning work we would have a cooked dinner and then bagin in the late afternoon before the second milking of the day, which was followed by a cooked tea. In short, although we didn't have much in the way of luxuries, we never went short of food and mum was certainly kept busy in the kitchen!

Even getting the cows ready for milking was a labour-intensive job in winter, that is, before we built the cow kennels (forerunners of modern cubicle buildings). Each cow was tied up in a stall (tied to a timber or concrete 'bostin' as we called it – known as 'boskin' in some parts of the country) and even though dad had created a collecting yard in the part of the main barn which adjoined our makeshift milking parlour (with a sliding door connecting the two), the cows still had to be untied and then driven through the yard and into the collecting area, then they all had to be tied up again after milking. Life was so much easier in summer, when the cows were out at pasture and not up for milking, but then it was important to keep an eye on each one when bringing them in for milking. First they had to be counted, which could be quite a tricky job until you got used to it, and they also had to be watched for any signs of lameness or of illness or distress, or for any signs of 'bulling', i.e. any signs of oestrus, which meant readiness for mating. In that case I reported to dad and he would ring and book a visit from the AI (artificial insemination) man.

One of the highlights of each year was when the cows were first let out to grass in the spring. They got very excited and would run around kicking their heels up behind them, just like young calves. Even though that sight was a very familiar one for us, we always looked forward to it every year. I suppose that was because, to us, it was a sure sign that spring really had arrived. On the other hand, it would be a complete revelation to non-farming folk, and

I remember that my wife Chris was amazed when she first saw it, and in fact she still mentions it to this day.

Turning-out time in spring also had its dangers, because we had to watch out for 'staggers' in the cows, a dramatic and potentially fatal condition caused by magnesium deficiency, which can occur at that time of year because fast-growing spring grass is too low in magnesium. The remedy is quite simple, an injection of a solution of magnesium and calcium under the skin of the cow in its shoulder area, which we would administer through a thick rubber tube from a large upturned bottle of the stuff (I think it was a pint). The needle was large and as a cow's skin is thick some force had to be used to get it through, but once that was done the job was easy and when all the solution was under the cow's skin it was simply a case of massaging the area to help the solution absorb quickly into the bloodstream. Like various other such tasks on the farm, this was something I learned to do simply by watching my dad.

Cows are herd animals and there is usually at least one ringleader in each group – the first one to break through a hedge or fence and to get somewhere it shouldn't be, often quickly followed by the rest of the herd.

That reminds me of the old story about a primary school teacher in a village school in a farming area who was trying to teach basic sums to a reception class. She asked Johnny, a farmer's son, how many sheep out of a flock of twenty would be left in a field if one of them escaped into the next field. When Johnny's answer was 'None', the teacher told him that he didn't know much about sums (I know, she wouldn't be allowed to say something like that today, so don't write in complaining) and Johnny's response was to point out that she didn't know much about sheep!

We eventually moved on to a self-feed silage system, with cow kennels and a slurry lagoon, so the farm needed very little in the way of machinery. We still kept Tiddley-Poo (registration UTF 310, by the way) which we used for scraping out and for till-sowing in spring, but contractors undertook the hedge-cutting and muck-spreading, as well as the cutting and carting of grass to the clamp when we were making silage. Dad paid a near neighbour, John Berry, to do the specialist job of buckraking the silage into a rectangular heap on our uncovered concrete pad (which we had laid ourselves – I can remember helping dad with that job one summer), ready for vacuum packing in a large sealed clamp. That I guess was partly due to the fact that John was good at the job, but mainly because we didn't possess a buckrake, let alone the push-off version which was needed for the job!

The slurry lagoon we had would never be allowed these days. The land was clay-based and contractors had used diggers to scrape off the topsoil, which they then banked up to form sides to the lagoon. Once a year, contractors would come with an excavator and a couple of very large tractors and spreaders and use the excavator to pull back part of the bank on one side of the lagoon, and to load the spreaders. The result was that they could complete all our muck-spreading for the year in less than two days. As you can imagine, the contractors were kept going by mum's regular administration of large quantities of food!

Of course, there was a cost involved, but it did mean that dad didn't need huge amounts of money tied up in expensive machinery which might have only been used for a few days each year at the very most. I think he must have worked it out! The arrangement was simple and crude, yet very cost-effective. However, I'm sure it must have caused a lot of pollution, because there was nothing to stop excess liquid (for want of a better expression) running into a nearby dyke (which I used to play in as a kid, and which I also later had to dig out by hand!).

Slurry lagoons can of course be very dangerous places, for

both animals and humans. We once had to rescue a calf from ours, after it had escaped from its pen and had managed to fall into the lagoon. Fortunately, the slurry wasn't too deep, because otherwise it could have drowned very quickly; but it couldn't move itself out, so a few of us had to perform a delicate operation to retrieve it. We found an old door, and by laying that on the surface, one of us (it might have been me, but I'm not sure it was) managed to crawl out and put a rope round the calf's neck, so we could pull it out. Happily, it was none the worse for its ordeal.

I also remember being told about some thieves who had been spotted on a farm near Out Rawcliffe, and who tried to make their escape by running across what they had clearly assumed was part of a field but which turned out to be the grass-covered crusty top of an open slurry lagoon! I believe the police wouldn't allow the miscreants into their car until a hosepipe had been used to wash them down from head to foot.

Before the slurry lagoon was constructed, that part of the farm had been a formal orchard. It still contained a number of apple and pear trees in particular, but many of them were quite ancient and didn't produce much fruit of any quality. However, the best fruit came from a line of Victoria plum trees which stood against a south-facing brick wall which was about 10 to 12 feet high and which was capped by huge sandstone blocks roughly 2 feet in width. Also, the plum trees were old and some of the branches had grown over and along the top of the wall in places. That meant that it was a challenging adventure for me as a young lad to climb up on top of the wall each autumn, then to crawl along it to reach the sweetest plums you have ever eaten (I can almost taste them now). The exercise wasn't without its dangers, however. Sweet plums attract wasps and we had them in very large numbers. They clearly resented anyone trying to get to the luscious fruit ahead of them, but that wasn't the only problem. The reason why the plums were so sweet was clearly the fact that not only did the trees stand in a sheltered position facing the sun, but they also had their feet in very rich manure. Remember the midden which I said earlier stood at one end of the yard? Well, that end of the yard was the other side of the said wall from the plum trees, and as I crawled precariously along the narrow top of the wall, with wasps buzzing angrily around my head as I tried to negotiate my way through the tangled branches, I could see the surface of the muck some 8 to 10 feet below me to my left. I'm sorry to disappoint you, but I never did fall into the midden! Having said that, I suppose that if that had ever happened, at least I would have had a soft landing!

I guess the legacy of those experiences is twofold. I still love Victoria plums (though they are never quite as sweet as the ones which grew above our midden), but I don't like wasps! In those days I would launch a single-handed campaign against the blighters every autumn, searching out their nests, which were often built into soft earth in hedgerow bottoms, then burning them. I would stuff newspaper into any nest I had located, douse it in diesel (of which we had plenty of course) and set fire to the lot. It was usually successful, but in those days I hadn't learned to wait until all the worker wasps had gone back into the nest at dusk before starting the operation, and the result was that I often got stung. I remember one occasion in particular when I was wearing an old rugby shirt which happened to have a hole under one armpit. You know what is coming next, don't you? Yes, you're right – one of the wasps found the hole and exacted its revenge – ouch!

A couple of other things about the old orchard come to mind. First, when I was very young, it contained about half a dozen cabins of various sizes, each filled with laying hens. At one time we also had hundreds of hens in various buildings around one of our two farmyards (they were actually cobbled courtyards with brick buildings on three sides), such as old stables, and the hens were even in lofts above some of those buildings. On the side of the first yard, the one nearer the farmhouse, were what had been two coach houses (which we used as garages), and running the length of the building above them was a long narrow loft which must have been used as a granary originally, because we knew it as 'the granary'. We kept hens in this 'granary' in battery cages that ran from one end to the other. It was a noisy, smelly place and not my favourite part of the farm. Access to the granary was via an external flight of stone steps at one end of the building. They were quite dangerous to use, because if there ever had been a rail along the edge of the steps it must have fallen off many years before. However, if you were being very adventurous, the steps, which strangely enough we knew as 'the granary steps', did afford access to the roof of the farmhouse kitchen (which was really a single-storey lean-to), or even to one of the bedrooms in the main part of the farmhouse.

Our egg production business didn't last too far into my childhood, for two reasons. First, all our hens had to be slaughtered (gassed) as a result of an outbreak of Fowl Pest. I think it happened in about 1964, so I would have been about ten. All the dead hens had to be taken out and buried in an open pit which had been dug in a field, another unpleasant job, which is probably why I have a clear memory of having to help. That episode was bad enough for us, but it was much worse for our neighbours, the Etherington family at Willow House Farm, because they had significantly more hens than us (ten thousand, I seem to recall). They all had to be slaughtered and buried too (the hens I mean, not the Etherington family!) and I remember helping them with that as well.

The other reason we didn't continue with egg production was that it became cheaper for us to buy eggs from someone else than to produce them ourselves, such was the state of the market at the time. Profits could clearly still be made from the egg production business even then, but only by those egg farms which operated on a large scale.

My other main memory about the orchard at the farm is that we held some major events there on Bonfire Night. By November we had usually amassed very large quantities of hedge cuttings from around the farm and we would use them to create a huge bonfire in the middle of the orchard. They would make a fantastic blaze, especially as the pile would always be doused with gallons of diesel. I can still remember large crowds of folk coming to enjoy the fun, and lots of us eating huge slabs of mum's homemade treacle toffee.

Dad ran a commercial (non-pedigree) dairy herd on a 'flying herd' basis. That meant that he didn't have to rear his own replacement heifers, but bought in new milk cows as and when he needed them. These usually replaced old cows which had been culled, or occasionally replaced ones which had become infertile for some reason or, worse still, had died (which fortunately didn't happen too often). That meant that he was subject to the market price when he had to buy in replacements, but I think he got most of the cows from the same dealer (a chap called Pennington if I remember correctly) with whom he had established a pretty good working relationship.

The fact that dad didn't have to rear dairy heifers in order to maintain his herd numbers did mean that he could use beef-breed bulls on his cows (always by artificial insemination – AI) and that gave him a very useful cash crop. In the sixties and seventies, semen from a number of continental beef breeds began to be imported into England. Dad cottoned on to that early on and he experimented with a few different breeds, such as Charolais, Simmental, Limousin and Blonde d'Aquitaine, before settling on Belgian Blues as his

First Blond d'Aquitaine calves born in the country through artificial insemination. Dad and cow, both proud of the twin calves.

favoured one. After our dad died, my sister Julie reminded me that he had achieved a measure of fame, getting his name and photo in the national farming press, when he had the first ever Blonde-cross calves (twins) bred by AI to be born in Britain.

Dad's Belgian Blue cross calves quickly gained a very good reputation in the local markets and he usually sold them at Brock Auction. He would keep them until they were two to three weeks old before taking them to market, by which time they had acquired a really good 'bloom' as he called it. Buyers from far and wide began to look out for dad's calves and as a result they attracted a premium price, so much so that a three-week-old bull calf would sell for as much as £250, even in those days!

So dad ran a very efficient operation. Like many farmers to this day he couldn't take time off, nor could he afford to be ill. He milked only about 35 cows, which wouldn't be anywhere near enough for a dairy farmer to make a living now, but dad was never in debt. With mum's help, of course, he brought up four children and although we never had money to spare, we had everything we needed.

Not a bad effort, I reckon!

As a kid growing up on the farm, I had the freedom to wander the fields and climb trees and to build a treehouse. It was more of a platform really, but it did give me a great view of any enemy forces which might choose to attack my position! In some ways it was an idyllic upbringing. As a little boy with two older sisters (as I said, Julie didn't make her appearance until I was nine) I had to make my own entertainment and amuse myself. I didn't mind that, because I had a good imagination and I was happy with my own company. Up to a point that is still true, because although I might appear to many to be a social animal, I do still enjoy being on my own. Having said that, when I was a little older, friends from school or from the village did come to the farm to play and we had some great adventures together.

Although the farm comprised only 45 acres it was still a fair distance from the farmstead to the farthest end of our land, which to us children seemed almost like another world. At that end of the farm the land ran downhill to a small field alongside Barton Brook, which is ultimately a tributary of the River Wyre. There were fish in it and dad had given permission to an angling club to fish the brook, in return for which they would bring us a present every Christmas. I was never interested in fishing, but when I was little my cousin Dave Butler (who was seven or eight years older than me) came a few times to fish and I remember him catching a brown trout once, as well as several eels. Many years later, a friend from grammar school, Mike Thomas, also came to fish at least once. The brook was certainly very clean then and I would sometimes stand in the shallows to try to spot stone loaches or sticklebacks, then I would try to catch them with my hands. Spotting the fish was fairly easy, but I never caught a single one!

Sometimes, if a few mates were with me, we would even swim in the deeper areas of our section of the brook (although I was never very good at swimming), or we would play in a small, sandy area which was almost a beach and occasionally we would take a picnic of sorts. There was a fair bit of sand down by the brook, so if we ever needed sand for any minor building projects on the farm we would take the tractor down to the brook and fill the transport box with it. It also meant that, as a toddler and beyond, I always had a good sandpit in the yard in which to play (except that the feral cats which lived in the lofts of the farm buildings did have a habit of using it as a toilet, which wasn't quite so nice).

A few fields downstream from our land, the Lancaster canal passes over the brook on an eighteenth-century aqueduct or – to put it the other way round – the brook passes underneath the canal, and it was a daring adventure for me and my friends to go there occasionally, especially as that involved us walking through fields owned by other farmers. I don't suppose we would have got into any trouble if we had been spotted, but I was always worried that it might happen.

A similar distance from our land, but in the other direction, was the railway. This was the West Coast mainline. To us, as youngsters in our early teens by then, it was an even greater adventure to go that way and to sneak up to the side of the tracks to watch the express trains go thundering past. The great thing was that some of them were still pulled by steam engines, and even more exciting was that along that particular section of line there were water troughs between the rails, from which the engines would scoop up water for their boilers while passing us at high speed, making water fly everywhere!

There was a wide variety of wildlife on the farm when I was a youngster, and I did genuinely appreciate it (most farming folk do, if truth be told). Multitudes of starlings (which we knew as 'shepsters' or 'sheppies', a name which I have now been told came from their habit of sitting on sheep) would gather on the farm buildings or on the wires running into them, and the chatter they made is one of the distinctive sounds that I associate with that part of my life. At night both barn owls and tawny owls could often be heard, but for me one of the greatest pleasures was to walk through a pasture on a hot summer's day and to listen out for a skylark singing. When I heard one I would lie down on my back to see if I could spot it soaring high above me. What an unforgettable sound that was! It actually prompted me to pen these words, when I was about 15 or 16 years old:

> *A lark*
> *thrills the heart*
> *from the azure beyond.*
> *This could be the start*
> *of a greater bond*
> *between man and God.*
> *Why not?*

I had my pocket edition of *The Observer's Book of Birds*, so I knew how to identify most of the birds I spotted around the farm, but one summer when I was about ten years old one particular bird that I had never come across before visited our neighbours' field for a few days. I never actually saw it, but the noise which was coming from the long grass in the field in question was clearly coming from a bird of some description. It was a sound I'd never heard before and which I have since heard only on television. It was very distinctive and unusual, almost like someone running

23

fingers across the teeth of a plastic comb. I consulted my book and decided that it could only be a corncrake. The next day I told my primary school headmaster what I had heard and he came down to the farm to hear for himself. When he heard the sound, he agreed with me that it could only be a corncrake.

Current-day 'twitchers' might view this story with a degree of scepticism, as I remember reading at the time that corncrakes were already very rare in England by then (and became extinct here quite soon after, I believe), but I knew what I had heard, and recent documentaries about corncrakes which have been on TV have served only to confirm my belief that I had indeed heard a corncrake in Woodplumpton in the mid-1960s. Furthermore, a twitcher I know well has recently told me that in the sixties corncrakes would have been passing through our area during their summer migration. So I was right after all.

My appreciation of nature included a love for some fantastic trees which stood on the farm, particularly in the front garden. Newsham Lodge had been built during the 1830s and was part of a small estate. Newsham Hall was the working farm, Newsham House, off Station Lane at Barton, was the gentleman's residence (sadly, it was demolished in the 1960s), and Newsham Lodge was built as a hunting lodge. It certainly wasn't grand when we lived there, but the house was very large. It comprised an impressive range of brick buildings (which included stables and coachhouses), the aforementioned large orchard, and in front of the house, facing south, what had clearly been a landscaped formal garden, with a good number of specimen trees. The signature tree was a very tall Chilean pine ('monkey puzzle' tree), which stood right in front of the house. All three of the main properties on the Newsham estate each had just such a tree.

The garden's days of splendour were long past when the Tomlinson family lived at Newsham Lodge, but at least the

Above: Newsham Lodge in the snow – note the granary steps.

Below: Carrying my sister Julie in a wheelbarrow in the garden at Newsham Lodge, 1965.

specimen trees were still there and they themselves were still splendid. They included a weeping ash, a copper beech, a lime and various yews and hollies, all of very impressive proportions. As a student revising for exams (probably my O-levels), I would sunbathe in the garden, looking up at these magnificent trees. Once again I was prompted to write a poem:

Three Trees

Towering stands our front garden copper beech
Casting dancing shadows on a summer lawn
Showering strands of colour fall and teach
When autumn comes, heralds of a new dawn.

Above and behind it stands an ageing lime
Its subtle shades reminding all the time
There is a form, indeed a plan
Behind nature, not guided by man.

And a yew, by comparison is stunted
And from its branches mice are hunted
By its perennial guest, owl, wise and old
Oh, if I but had the lips, the glory to be told!

The house was far less romantic, especially in winter. There was no central heating, just coal or wood fires and a back boiler heated by the solid fuel stove/range in the kitchen. There was no plumbing at all upstairs and the only toilet was outside, near the back door. Sometimes during winter we had to leave a paraffin heater lit in it to stop the pipes freezing. There was a bathroom on the ground floor (which had clearly been added by the erection of a timber partition down what had probably been a very grand passageway), but it was a long (though necessarily very speedy) run to it from the bedrooms on a cold winter morning. We all learned to get dressed very quickly in winter, even under the bedclothes sometimes, and I honestly do remember having to scrape ice off the inside of my bedroom window before I could look out on some winter mornings.

Fortunately, the stove/range in the kitchen (it was a Rayburn) was a very reliable source of hot water, although we had to ensure that the fire never went out. It had a fire door at the front which we could open, so before going out to work on cold mornings we would often sit on a stool in front of the open fire door and warm our toes over the fire before pulling on our wellies and venturing outside. However, mum would go one further than that. I can picture her now, standing with her back against the rail which ran across the front of the stove, with the fire door open and her skirt raised at the back, warming her bottom in the heat of the flames!

As soon as I was old enough I was expected to help on the farm. My jobs increased as I moved into my teens. I don't remember objecting, but simply accepted that that was what was required.

People do sometimes ask if I ever wanted to be a farmer myself. The answer is no. When I was about eleven I realised that I didn't want to milk cows every day for the rest of my life. I have always understood that some farmers absolutely love the whole science of animal husbandry and how improving their stock can be a life's work for them, but I never felt like that.

I have learned that some of the best farming partnerships, between brothers for example, are those in which one partner is the stockman and the other loves machinery, but I didn't have any desire for that either. For me, when I was in a milking parlour I was bored and felt that I might just as well have been in a factory.

I had the academic ability that gave me the opportunity to make different life-choices, although at that stage I had no idea what they might be. To his credit dad never tried to force me (or any of my sisters) into farming, probably because of his own experience as a young man. My sister Julie was involved in farming for a while, but that was her choice. She was a member of Young Farmers (I never was, although ironically later in my career I did serve for three years as a trustee of the Lancashire County Federation of Young Farmers' Clubs) and she worked as a milk recorder for a while. Her first marriage was to a farmer, Ian Metcalf, and both their sons, Sam and Joe, are now working with Ian on his farm.

The result is that there are no longer any members of our particular branch of the Tomlinson clan still involved in farming. When people ask if I am related to certain farming Tomlinsons in or around the Fylde area, I always explain that there are two Tomlinson farming families in the area, the rich ones and the poor ones, and that we were the poor ones! It is of course ironic in some ways that I have ended up spending virtually all of my professional career acting for farmers, but even that family connection with the industry is ending now.

For her part, mum just wanted all her children to do well, which I suppose is what any mother would desire. She was always very proud when any of us achieved anything. In a way, that was also slightly sad because mum didn't have many other interests and as she got older her conversations were nearly always about the achievements of her children and later her grandchildren.

So these are my roots. We were farmers, not wealthy and I guess you would say lower middle class, but I had a happy childhood in a stable and fairly happy family. I had to work hard, but I never lacked anything I needed and I'm sure that all of that gave me a very solid foundation for what was yet to come.

CHAPTER TWO

IN A FIELD NEAR WHITBY

A decision that defined me

When I was twelve a farmer's son from our village, Geoff Parkinson, started a new youth group at the parish church. He had gone up to Oxford University and while there he had become a Christian through contact with a Church of England youth organisation for 11 to 15 year olds known as Pathfinders. Geoff came home to Preston to start a teaching career (he later moved into banking) and got permission from the vicar at the time, George Jackson (a very nice chap but ineffectual), to start a Pathfinder group in the village. I became one of the founder members and we would meet in the village school at 9.30 for an hour every Sunday morning.

I tagged along with some of my contemporaries and realised that I quite enjoyed it. There were quizzes and competitions, which suited my competitive nature. There was 'God stuff' too, such as 'memory verses' to learn, and always a little talk, which was in effect a mini sermon. I didn't mind it, although initially it made no impression on me. That was in the autumn of 1966.

The following year Geoff took some of us to a boys' summer camp near Whitby on the Yorkshire coast. It was in a field at Deep Grove Farm in the village of Lythe, behind the top of the spectacular cliffs which are just up the coast from the lovely seaside village of Sandsend. It was a beautiful spot and it's still worth a visit. Our route down to the beach was via a section of what had been a cliff-top railway which led to some quarries behind the cliffs. I believe some sections of that have since fallen into the sea and the path has had to be diverted.

I revisited Deep Grove Farm about eight years later, after my final exams at Durham University. We had about three weeks free before term finished, so one of my college friends, John Parkin, suggested we make time for an adventure. Of course, I agreed. John borrowed a tandem bike from one of his lecturers, and off we cycled, all the way to Whitby and back, carrying a tent and a few basic provisions on the back of the bike. It was about 60 miles in each direction, but we were away for only two nights. The first night we pitched our tent after dark on the North York Moors (next to a 'No Camping' sign!) and the second night we paid to camp at Deep Grove Farm, which at least had the luxury of a toilet for the use of campers.

I remember that we hardly slept during the first night, and that we woke very early. It was a beautiful summer morning, so we struck camp and decided to resume our journey into Whitby. That turned out to be a very memorable hour or so. There was low mist hanging over the fields as we pedalled through glorious pastoral scenery on an empty road along the bottom of a valley. We climbed our way up out of the valley and onto the main road and whizzed down the hill into Whitby itself. That part of the journey was exhilarating! The roads had remained quiet and the tandem, being an old-fashioned one, was quite heavy, so we were able to muster a considerable speed to freewheel downhill for the last two or three miles, banking around roundabouts as we did so. When we finally arrived at the harbour side we were in time to see the fishing boats coming in loaded with their catches, and their crews making their way to the quayside butty van. We joined them and shared with them in the sheer joy of a steaming mug of tea and a bacon sandwich.

Back in August 1967 the camping at the Pathfinder camp was very well organised, but basic. We slept in bell tents, in groups of six or so, each with an adult tent leader, and the organisation of the camp was along quasi-military lines, with the leaders taking titles like Adjutant, Quartermaster and Camp Commandant (or 'commie'!). That year, the commie was a chap by the name of Dick Cotton who wore knee-length khaki shorts all the time. The facilities were rudimentary, with soil latrines and toilet tents with buckets which had to be emptied into a soil pit. That lovely job fell to the 'junior officers', teenagers who were too old to be official 'campers' but not old enough to be leaders, yet had volunteered to help out. I did that myself for a few years and, believe it or not, it was a lot of fun. We junior officers were allotted our own tent. There were opportunities for us to fraternise with some of the cooks, who were about our own age and the only females on the site. We were overseen by an officer with the splendid title of 'JOK', which stood for 'Junior Officer Keeper'. We were all basically good lads but it was probably still an apt title – for example, I remember sneaking out of the tent late at night to rendezvous with some of the cooks and some of us going for moonlight walks along the cliff top. It was harmless stuff, but in those days it was nonetheless exciting.

A large group from a Baptist church in Banbury in Oxfordshire came to the camps for a good number of years. This group included a girl called Stella, whom I fancied at the time, but also a lad called

Ken Taylor and another girl by the name of Caroline. I became good friends with Ken and Caroline and when they got married in Banbury in 1974 I had the great pleasure of being Ken's best man. The couple have since lived in Ottery St Mary in Devon for very many years, and they have always kept in touch with my family.

Once or twice I also went on the 'Advance Party' before a Pathfinder Camp at Sandsend. That involved joining a group who would set up the marquee and the cooking tents, as well as digging the latrines and soil pit and setting up the toilet tents. That was all very well, but the really unpleasant job came if you were in the 'Rear Party' who dismantled everything at the end of the week's camp and were nominated to fill in the soil pit. It was less of a problem for me than for some of the others because, in a way, I had grown used to that kind of thing at home on the farm.

Everyone on the camp had to wash using cold water out in the open, although the female cooks were allowed to wash inside their tents and I believe they were allowed to use some of the camp's very limited supply of hot water. A tin mug full of hot water could also usually be had by the men and lads who actually needed to shave and wanted to bother! If we needed more than a wash the remedy was that the whole camp would troop down to the beach for a dip in the sea.

Although all of this was very strange to me at first (I'm sure I had never been camping before that) I soon grew to love the annual camps and I became a regular for many years, graduating in time to become one of the leaders and then getting involved with the planning of the camps. We arranged countless games and sports into a variety of competitions (all of which was right up my street), and these events were brought together to form an overall competition between the four teams of campers led by their respective leaders. Each team was usually asked to compose a team chant or song, which involved much hilarity and fun for all. We sat round campfires, enjoyed barbeques and sang at camp concerts. Then, every year, the whole camp would go off site for a day trip by bus, to somewhere like Scarborough or York, or Whitby. The buses, which were all red, were run by a company called United and they were ancient, noisy and very slow. Think of the television series *Heartbeat* and you will get the picture.

Group of youths on a day trip to Scarborough from Pathfinder camp circa 1967; Graham Duncan is on the wall with Claude Rollins behind him.

On the Sunday morning of every week-long camp we would all walk the half-mile or so to Lythe Church, which was on the main road next to the entrance to the farm road leading to Deep Grove Farm. Some of the leaders and sometimes even the campers would take part in the morning service, singing or reading. Some of the leaders occasionally preached too.

There were boys who joined in this camp from all over the north of England, and others from the Midlands. Some hailed from challenging situations in inner cities (in those days we would have called them 'rough' backgrounds), and it was at Sandsend that I met a non-white boy for the very first time. He was of West Indian heritage and I think his name was Claude Rollins (where are you now, Claude?). He was a very nice lad and an excellent footballer.

The evening meetings at the camps were held in the camp marquee, beneath the light cast from Tilley lamps, and concluded with a mug of watery cocoa before bedtime. These sessions did, of course, include 'God stuff'. We would sing Christian songs and choruses, listen as one of the leaders talked to us, and then retire to our tents where the tent leader (sometimes assisted by one of the junior officers) would lead us in a 'quiet time', which involved reading the Bible and praying. As you can well imagine, some of the lads were more co-operative than others! That was all new to me, but I just accepted it because it was, after all, a camp being run by a church organisation. But then, as the week progressed on that first camp for me, the things I was hearing in the evening meetings and in the quiet times began to start sounding right. There came a point when we were all challenged in one of the meetings to 'become Christians' by praying a prayer of confession and commitment to God. I don't know why or how, but suddenly it really did all make sense. It wasn't an emotional thing for me. I simply weighed it all up on an intellectual basis and decided that what I was being told must be true and that if it was, I had better commit myself to it. So that's exactly what I did.

There was no flash of lightning or peel of thunder. It just felt right. When I woke the following morning it still felt right. I knew then that I would never be the same person again, and also that God would never allow anyone to 'pluck me out of His hand', meaning that I would always be a Christian until my dying day.

Since that memorable Tuesday in August 1967, being a Christian is what has defined me, Geoff Tomlinson, farmer's son and solicitor, as a person. My priorities changed immediately. Something I noticed almost at once was that the really bad temper I'd had up until then disappeared (for the most part). I had had a tendency to operate on a very short fuse, but suddenly I realised that I could keep my temper in its place. Cynics might say that that happened because I was trying very hard and I guess there may be some truth in that, but it wasn't just a temporary thing. I am sure that I have recognised the work of the Holy Spirit in my life – whether or not anyone else has seen that is another matter, but that's not for me to judge.

I do still get annoyed, of course I do, but *I hope* that is limited to times when I encounter things like injustice or unjustified obstinacy. Oh, and cyclists who don't think the Highway Code applies to them… but that's another story!

The fact that I have been a Christian since I was thirteen does not mean for one moment that I have led a blameless life. Far from it, in fact. There have been periods in my life when I have done things which I would be ashamed to share and which I do not want to discuss. I would not want to pretend otherwise. The main thing is that I know that I am forgiven and I move onwards. Where the rubber hits the road, it is true that the decision I made in 1967 has continued to give me purpose in life and a deep, deep satisfaction.

As an adult I wanted to marry a Christian woman, and eventually I was able to do that. Our faith then influenced the way we sought to bring up our children, and it has also dictated many of my activities outside work. I have been involved in many Christian organisations as well as attending church most Sundays, but I have also been heavily involved in both watching and playing various sports, particularly rugby when I was younger, and now golf.

Becoming a Christian doesn't mean that you immediately acquire an identikit Christian personality. I still have my own personal characteristics just like everyone else (and my faults –

I've often said that I am very well aware of my shortcomings, because my wonderful wife reminds me of them on a daily basis!), but the difference for me is that I have a reason for not reacting like Pavlov's dog to certain stimuli (or temptations if you like), and I believe that God helps me in this way.

I hope that for those of you who know me, hearing of my Christian faith will not come as a surprise to you. If it has, I must have got a lot wrong over the years, for which I apologise. Maybe for others the revelations concerning my Christian faith and behaviour have clarified or explained some of the things you have noticed about me over the years. I do hope so.

CHAPTER THREE

GEOFF WAS A GRAFTER

My Education

I attended Kirkham Grammar School (KGS) between 1965 and 1972. One of the real characters there at that time was a biology teacher named Fred Sayer. He was newly qualified when I was in his O-level class, but he stayed at KGS for the rest of his career, so he eventually ended up teaching my son Andy. Because he was the newest teacher, Fred had been assigned the 'non-scientist' pupils, that is the boys who were majoring in arts subjects and for whom biology was the only science subject for which they would sit an O-level exam. I was in that category.

Some years later, I was playing for the Old Boys' cricket team against the school first XI and Fred Sayer was one of the umpires. That day, my good friend Keith Aitchison was captain of the Old Boys' team. The school team batted first but they began to lose wickets on a regular basis. Keith knew that I liked to bowl a bit, but from my position fielding on the boundary I began to wonder if I would get a chance to bowl before the school team were all out.

As it happened, when I did come on to bowl there was only one wicket left to fall, and I was to bowl from the end at which Fred was standing.

In typical extrovert fashion Fred gave me a big build-up, announcing to everyone on the field of play, and probably to anyone far further afield within earshot, that I had been the first ever student of his to gain a grade 1 pass in biology at O-level. Thanks, Fred!

And guess what? I bowled the last man with my first ball!

Many years after that, my wife and I spoke to Fred one parents' evening. Our son Andy was then in Fred's class and obviously we were enquiring about his progress. Very astutely, Fred told us that Andy was far brighter than me (which is true) but, he added, 'Geoff was a grafter.'

I realise that what Fred Sayer said that evening was an accurate analysis of my approach to most things in life. I have a certain level of academic ability, but the main thing about me is that I have always been very conscientious and a hard worker. Whatever else might be said about me, I have never lacked determination, nor indeed its intimate bedfellow, optimism.

While I would certainly not claim that all of the following quote applies to me, I do like this definition of optimism by Pastor Dietrich Bonhoeffer which I came across recently:

> *'The essence of optimism is that it takes no account of the present, but it is a source of inspiration, of vitality and hope where others have resigned. It enables a man to hold his head high, to claim the future for himself and not to abandon it to his enemy.'*

Another quote I like, ascribed to German artist Herm Albright (1876–1944), is:

'A positive attitude may not solve all your problems, but it will annoy enough people to make it worth the effort.'

St Anne's Woodplumpton Church of England Primary School, 1959–1965

I started school at the age of four, attending the village school with my two older sisters Jen and Kath. My younger sister Julie followed nine years later (as she would tell you, she was 'an afterthought'!). From the very beginning I was eager to please and I think I must have enjoyed school work because I was soon doing well. It was a small village school and before long I was moved up to the class above my age group. One classmate in that group was Kath Cope (née Harding), and we are still good friends to this day, well over fifty years later.

I passed the eleven-plus exam at the age of ten, but the headmaster, Eric Sagar, very wisely discouraged my parents from sending me to grammar school a year early, so during my final year at Woodplumpton School I often received one-to-one tuition from him. He was something of a scholar; and I remember that he had me reading Tennyson!

I can't remember all that much more about my primary school days, although I can recall being very keen on football as well as being a reasonably good runner. I believe I was generally happy, although even at that early age I did occasionally worry that the continuing Cold War would lead to a nuclear holocaust and the end of the world. In my childlike way I was quite frightened by that prospect.

In November 1963 one incident which sticks clearly in my mind occurred when I was at an evening function of some sort, in the school hall. Mr Sagar interrupted proceedings to announce that he had just heard that President John F. Kennedy had been assassinated. Many people who were alive then will tell you that they know exactly where they were when that momentous event in history happened; that certainly applies to me.

That extra year of primary school definitely stood me in good stead when I eventually moved on to Kirkham Grammar School.

Kirkham Grammar School, 1965–1972

I'm sure going to the 'big school' must have been just the same sort of experience for thousands of children both before and after me, but it was daunting for me at first. That was especially so because I had to catch a service bus into Preston bus station and then another service bus out to Kirkham. The journey took the best part of an hour at each end of the day, and all this for an eleven-year-old boy who had never been on a bus journey on his own before then. Of course, I soon coped with that trauma and adapted to the newness and size of the school (which seemed very big compared to the village primary but in fact registered only about 350 pupils), and I quickly settled in and started to make friends.

I focused well on my studies and was quickly established at or near the top of my class in most subjects. I wasn't quite top overall, but I became determined to achieve that, and my old school report book (which I still have) shows that I managed it in the second year. After that I think I became bored and I started to mess around in class a bit, so academically I went through a lull for a couple of years. There was nothing too dramatic though and I did stay near the top of the class and knuckled down when I had to, in due course getting nine good O-level passes, two of them when I was 15 and in the fourth year.

One problem with KGS was that O-level options had to be decided before the end of the third year (at the tender age of 14) and, presumably because the school was modest in size, the curriculum was such that studying a combination of arts and science subjects wasn't an option. That meant that I had to decide one way or the other at that relatively early stage. The difficulty for me was that I had been doing well at science subjects (because I was blessed with a good memory for facts) but marginally better at arts subjects. On that basis alone I chose arts subjects, which is why I took only one science subject at O-level, as mentioned above. That effectively determined my A-level subjects, which were history, geography and French. This closed the door on one possible career which I had tentatively considered up to that point, which was medicine. How different my life would have been had I become a doctor!

Incidentally, the fact that I have always had a good memory (until now at least!) may also explain why I have been able to bore so many people over the years with countless terrible jokes which have lodged in my mind. Do I owe you an apology for that? On the other hand it has come in useful in pub quizzes, which I still enjoy.

I had some good friends at school and I am still in touch with one or two (notably Andrew Townsend), and I do see others occasionally. I seemed to be reasonably popular and, insofar as there was such a thing, I guess I was one of the 'in crowd'. One of my best friends had been Rob Fisher, but we lost touch completely when he went off to Southampton University to study chemical engineering, and then emigrated to the USA to work in the oil industry. As far as I know, Rob is still there.

One of the really weird things about KGS was that, during my first five years there, not only did we still have to wear school caps but we actually also still had regular school on Saturday mornings. That was especially awkward for me because I still had to make the arduous bus journey both ways and the buses were less regular on Saturdays. I think we were at school from 9.00am until 12.00 noon each Saturday, so at best I arrived home at 1.30pm. It was a real treat when, on a rare occasion, one of my parents drove to school to collect me.

The deal was that in return for going to school on Saturdays we got longer holidays than most other schools. That was all very well, but it wasn't much use when my mates from home went to other schools, so were not around when I wanted to meet up with them!

The Saturday morning school thing was also awkward if, like me, you were playing for a school rugby team on the Saturday afternoon, which was the norm then (although we also played some matches on Wednesday afternoons). There was obviously not enough time to go home and back after school, so to get some lunch there was no choice but to walk into Kirkham to buy fish and chips (from the Lane Ends Chippie, which is still there to this day). The one concession was that the school would allow us to take our meals back to school and eat them in the canteen – big deal!

Rob Fisher (or more accurately, his mum) came to the rescue after a while because, although Rob wasn't in the rugby team (he excelled at summer sports and he was a very good cricketer), I was invited to their house for lunch every Saturday when I had to stay on after school. They lived in Wesham, so it was probably the best part of a mile to their house, but it didn't take long to walk there and back and I was never late for a match. The only possible downside was that Mrs Fisher always made us a full roast lunch every time, a vast improvement on fish and chips but definitely not the best sort of meal to eat before a rugby match, not that I noticed at the time. It was incredibly kind of the Fisher family and I still think about their generous hospitality even after all these years.

Sport featured highly at KGS, which suited me, although at first I was disappointed that it was a rugby-playing school, because football was my first love. However, I soon began to enjoy rugby, becoming fairly good at it and securing a place in the school under-12s team. I won't say any more here about my career in school sports, because I deal with that and other sports in chapter ten.

As a school, KGS followed numerous traditions, which is not surprising given that it was founded in 1549. My family played a small part in the school's history in the sense that I was the third generation of Tomlinsons to attend, following my grandad John (Jack) and my dad Ralph. I mentioned previously that our son Andy also went there, although KGS was very different by then, having reverted to fully independent status. In my time it was an old-fashioned boys' grammar school, with an emphasis on traditional subjects (including Latin, which I did at O-level) and sports, and teachers who wore academic gowns to assemblies and lessons. We also had a fearsome headmaster called W.H. (Bill) Kennedy – a huge man with a military bearing (complete with military moustache) and a frightening temper, who could and would administer frightful canings. You simply did not want to get on the wrong side of him. I was sufficiently astute to avoid that; nevertheless I was scared stiff and I'm sure I wasn't the only one.

Looking back to that era, I think that the level of teaching at KGS was quite poor. Some of the staff were really nice chaps, it's true, but even then it seemed clear to me that many of them had simply been given teaching jobs after leaving the forces and that they had no teaching qualifications at all. There were also one or two who just could not control a class or keep any kind of discipline, but they fell by the wayside pretty quickly and left. Some of the staff were more like pantomime characters than respected teachers from whom we felt we were likely to learn something important. So the general standard of teaching at KGS in my time was pretty low. There was a good spirit within the school, but there was little or no support for the general welfare of pupils.

However, there were a few excellent teachers. One of them was 'Butch' Knowles who taught geography (I never knew his first name). Others were Bernard ('Bernie') Coates who taught history, and Harry Reay who taught French. Harry Reay had a daughter called Barbara who was about the same age as me. Two things about Barbara: one was that she went out with my friend Rob Fisher for a while, and the other was that her nickname was 'the Gin Palace Queen'! *(Why, I don't know!)* I was lucky in that I had three good teachers tutoring me through my A-levels, but on reflection that may be why I chose those subjects!

KGS was a 'boys only' school, so for most of the time we were starved of female company, but when we reached the ages of about 15 or 16 my mates and I did manage to get to know one or two girls from other schools, usually Kirkham girls who went to girls' schools like Queen Mary's in Lytham, or Elmslie in Blackpool, or even to The Park School in Preston. It helped that one or two of them would get off their school buses right in front of KGS. One girl I remember as being tall and attractive was called Lynn Pemberton. I did 'go out' with another Kirkham girl for a while when I was about 15 or 16, Lynn Parkinson. She was also quite tall and I think I met her at the Kirkham Methodist Youth Club, which I used to attend on Friday nights along with some of my school friends, including Rob Fisher. Lynn Parkinson always looked really good in the very short miniskirts that were in fashion back then. She eventually married a lad from my year at KGS called Mick Eccles, but sadly she later died of cancer at quite a young age.

Another girlfriend from my teens was Angela France, who was also part of the same youth-club gang. To me, she had all the advantages of being a farmer's daughter, and a Christian, as well as being pretty and a lot of fun. I was really stuck on her, but it didn't work out (actually, she broke my heart – but that's another story). We did keep in touch for a few years after Angela dumped me, and she once even visited me at university. I was still holding out hope then that something might still happen between us, but Angela met someone else at teacher training college, and by now they must have been married for about forty years.

When I was 17 and in the Upper Sixth at KGS there was a terrible tragedy in Kirkham which affected a lot of people, and especially those connected with the Methodist Youth Club, which I was still attending at the time. A Kirkham girl who was the same age as me and a stalwart of that club, Elizabeth Foster, disappeared. Her body was found a day or two later (I think she had been dumped near a track on farmland near Wrea Green), and a murder enquiry began. Every male who had had any connection with Liz was interviewed, and that included me. The police came to our farm to examine the tread on the farm van which I was driving by then. Because my friend Rob Fisher had been the only proper boyfriend Liz had had, he became the prime suspect for a while, which must have caused him extreme stress, until a local bus driver was eventually arrested and convicted.

Liz was a committed and enthusiastic Christian, as were her parents. Naturally, her tragic death had a profound effect on a lot of people. I went to the funeral and it was an emotional affair, but the attitude and strength of character from all concerned presented an incredibly strong Christian witness to everyone who was involved.

One of the people most deeply affected by the whole affair was Ken Leech, a police officer who had been involved in the investigation. His interactions with people led him to consider matters of faith and eventually, with the encouragement of his mother, he decided to become a Christian, later leaving the force to enter into full-time ministry as a pastor in the Free Methodist denomination. I got to know Ken quite well. In 1994 he became the superintendent of the Great Britain and Northern Ireland Conference of Free Methodist Churches. Tragically, Ken himself was killed in an air accident on an internal flight in the USA, while travelling on church business. He had written a fascinating and moving story of the murder investigation, his conversion and life. After the accident his wife Joan helped to update it, and *Dark Providence, Bright Promise*, published by Light and Life Press, is still available from Google Books.

Back at school, A-levels eventually came and went and I was disappointed, if not embarrassed, when I messed up my history papers and got a D, because it really was my strongest subject. Fortunately, the two Bs I gained in geography and French were sufficient to see me onto my chosen university course, to study law at Durham. I know I was lucky and that under the current selection system it would have been a very different story.

It was Bernie Coates, my history teacher, who was responsible both for my application to Durham and also for my choice of law as my subject. He was a scholarly chap who shared much invaluable wisdom with his students. He himself had been at Grey College, Durham and encouraged me to follow in the footsteps of a recent head boy (Captain of the School), Dave Cowell, who was already attending Grey College. That sounded good to me, mainly because Dave was a good rugby player, and indeed someone whom I had admired in his time at KGS.

The suggestion that I should consider studying law was made by Bernie on what I am sure was a common basis, namely that studying law would be a good academic discipline which would stand me in good stead later on, even if I did not eventually decide to follow a career in the law. I suspect that that is also the reason why law is still one of the most popular subjects at university.

I don't know to this day whether or not Bernie put in a good word for me at Grey (although I suspect that he may have done so, because the then Master of the college had been a contemporary of Bernie's at Grey and I think they were still good friends). In any event, after following the proper application process I landed a very early interview, followed by the generous offer of a place to read law, subject to my being awarded only two B-grade passes in my A-levels.

The procedure actually involved undertaking two separate interviews, one in the law department and the other in Grey College. Travelling to Durham for those interviews was an exciting yet daunting experience for a country boy like me. I had to negotiate my way there by train (changing at York), which I think was my first ever train journey alone. On arriving at Durham, the arrangement was that interviewees stayed in the college overnight, another new experience and quite strange. I searched out Dave Cowell, who was very kind and supportive. I remember thinking how sophisticated it felt to share sherry in his room before the evening meal (dinner).

I liked Durham instantly and knew that I really wanted to be a part of the life there. Apart from the history and beauty of the place, the university would provide many opportunities for sport, especially rugby, and there was a very strong and active Christian Union. Roll on Durham, I thought!

The offer I had received was very generous, even for 1971, so the pressure was off me in a sense, but after that early offer I then received rejections from all the other universities to which I had applied, which was a little disconcerting. I reasoned to myself that the other universities must have known that Durham really wanted me and that they had therefore decided that there would be no point in offering me anything. That was a bit rash, I know, but nevertheless I took the precaution of applying to a polytechnic as well. In those days the polytechnics ran a separate application system and I went to Nottingham for an interview to read law at

Trent Polytechnic. I duly received an offer but, to me, it wasn't an appealing institution and I am not sure if I would have taken it up had I failed to get into Durham.

I drove to Nottingham for the interview and remember taking with me a lad from my year at KGS who had an interview at Trent on the same day. His name was Gareth Suttle and he was a boarder at KGS, even though his home was not all that far away at Maghull on Merseyside. I don't think Gareth did go to Trent in the end because he emigrated to New Zealand with his family and I believe he left for New Zealand straight after leaving KGS. He was a friendly lad and I sometimes wonder what became of him. We broke the journey to Nottingham by calling on the Tomlinson family at Ashover in Derbyshire, which was quite a treat for me, but the Tomlinsons were not quite so sure at first because, as they told us later, when they saw two young men in suits walking into the farmyard they thought we were Jehovah's Witnesses!

I think most of my failed university applications were also to read law, but I do remember that one of them was for politics and modern history at Manchester. I also remember preferring the idea of going to a university sufficiently far away from home but still in the north of England, so of course Durham fitted that bill perfectly. Earlier, I had decided that I would not apply to Oxford or Cambridge, and in any event I very much doubt I would have got into either of those prestigious universities, although I got the impression that KGS wanted me to apply to Oxford. I guess I was something of an inverted snob, or perhaps somewhat self-conscious of my roots as a farmer's son from a lower middle-class northern background. That kind of thinking was obviously nonsensical, but back then I knew no better.

There was also a perception that Durham was the university of

GEOFF WAS A GRAFTER

choice for any Oxbridge rejects, but I had made Durham my first choice and they wanted me, which was good enough for me.

I did get something of a shock when I arrived at Durham in early October 1972 because the university undergraduate population as a whole was said to be about fifty percent ex-public school, and in one new college called Collingwood, which opened during my time in Durham, the figure was higher, apparently sixty-five percent!

Before I talk about my university days I have a few more thoughts to mention about my school, Kirkham Grammar. KGS was a good foundation for Durham with its traditional set-up, which included six 'houses', affording plenty of opportunity for competition in a variety of areas of school life. That suited my competitive nature. There was School House, which was for the limited number of boarders at the school, and five other 'houses', all loosely based on geographical locations, namely Kirkham, Fylde, Preston, Ashton and Lytham. Each house had its own separate assembly every week, with a senior teacher acting as 'House Master' and a member of the Upper Sixth appointed as 'House Captain'.

Because I lived near Preston I should really have been in Preston House, but as my grandfather and father had both been in Fylde House my parents applied for me to be in Fylde, and that's what happened. Following in my dad's footsteps I eventually became House Captain. Our son Andy was also in Fylde when he was at KGS, so the family tradition was continued.

Overall, and with the benefit of long hindsight, I am sure I would have done just as well at any other grammar school in the area – there were plenty to choose from in those days.

The sport was good but I grew up to realise that it was not as good as I had thought at the time. I came to understand that I had my own limitations as a rugby player, but I also believe that

I could have become a better player if I'd had the benefit of some individual coaching when I was at school. The head of games then, Dave Worth, was a good club player himself, a winger for both Fylde and Preston Grasshoppers, and some years later I did end up playing with him at Preston. Nowadays I regard him as a friend. So it will make you smile when you see what Dave wrote on my end-of-season report; the story is that while playing full-back for the first team during my last year at school, I had decided that as I was the last line of defence I would concentrate on ensuring that my defensive play was up to scratch. That must have worked because in my end-of-season report Dave wrote, '*He has developed during the term as a very safe full-back, particularly as a tackler*', but then continued, '*Geoff could perhaps develop his attacking play to a higher level and try to link more with the three-quarters.*' The problem was that he had never once said that to me during the season. He was the coach, so how was I supposed to know that kind of thing if he didn't tell me? Could have done better, Mr Worth!

Having said all that, the summer after I left school I did some training at Fylde Rugby Club with Glen Leeming, the hooker in our school team, who went on to become a Fylde stalwart. I wasn't sure whether to join Fylde or Preston Grasshoppers and when I asked Dave for his advice he pointed me very firmly towards Preston, which as it turned out, was absolutely the right club for me.

For a good number of years after I left school I was an active member of the Old Boys' Association, which became the Old Kirkhamians when the school became mixed, and I followed my dad by becoming President of the Association. I was also a regular participant in the annual rugby match which the Old Boys were then allowed to hold against the school first team. Also, a couple of times, I played cricket matches against the school. Just after

Andy had left KGS the three of us all attended the annual dinner, where our photograph was taken, three generations of Tomlinsons together, something which really pleased dad in particular.

Durham University, 1972–1975

The best years of my life? In many ways I think they were. I found independence, new friends, lots of rugby, a very good Christian Union and an interesting (though demanding) degree course, all set in a beautiful small city.

I genuinely loved my time at university. Looking back, I realise how privileged I was, not least because everything was free. We didn't have to pay tuition fees and most students also received a maintenance grant from their local authority. For two of my three years as an undergraduate my parents didn't earn enough for me not to qualify for a full grant, and in the other year they made up the shortfall. I continued to work at home on the farm during university vacations, for which I did get paid some pocket money. One year when dad didn't have enough work for me (or perhaps he couldn't afford to pay me), I spent a few weeks working at Cutts Lane Nurseries, Out Rawcliffe, which was owned and run by the in-laws of my sister Jen.

When I started at university it was all a completely new experience for me (as for everyone else, I suppose), but I was definitely happy to be stepping out on the road to full independence.

Durham is a collegiate university, but the colleges are really no more than glorified halls of residence, although (in my time there at least) each one did have its own distinct identity and culture. Grey College had several uninspiring residential blocks which were built in the 1960s, and which some have described as resembling council houses from that era. Construction of the college was apparently started in 1959, only for it to burn down, which explains the presence on the college crest of a pair of fireman's ladders. The college was named after Earl Grey, who was Prime Minister when Durham University was founded in 1832. Although its architecture was uninspiring, Grey did have the considerable advantage of being situated in an excellent location on the south side of Durham city, which offered the residents a wonderful view down the hill to the cathedral and castle in the city centre, where they nestle within a long loop of the River Wear.

In my time, Grey College was all male, although that has since changed. The arrangements were that each student was allocated a study bedroom which he kept for the whole of the first year, but then moved to a different one for years two and three, except that for one of the three terms in year two every student was required to share a double room with another undergraduate. There was an option to live out of college for those who preferred to live more independently and could be bothered to find their own digs, but Durham differed from most universities in those days in that there was enough accommodation available in colleges for the majority of undergraduates to be able to 'live in' for all three years if they wished. To me, that seemed a sensible and easy option, so I never really contemplated living out of the college environment.

The rooms were not en suite in those days – we hadn't even heard the expression 'en suite' then! Toilets and showers were located at the end of most corridors. There was also a television room and a snooker room, and I think there were telephone kiosks in each block – and of course, mobile phones were not invented! This meant that, apart from emergencies, contact with home or with distant girlfriends was usually via handwritten letter (remember those?). No doubt the girlfriends received more letters than our parents…

There were several flats within the college buildings, which were usually occupied by live-in lecturers, mainly the unmarried ones. Three meals a day were provided in college as part of what was on offer for the fees (which I was easily able to pay out of my maintenance grant) and they weren't bad at all. In fact, in my first two years we even had the option of a cooked breakfast every morning! Meals were taken in a large communal dining hall, which was also where college dances and balls took place. Most meals were informal cafeteria-style affairs, but once a week there would be a formal dinner at which we all had to wear an academic gown (over our jeans and tee-shirts) and sat on long benches at long wooden tables. Grace was also said in Latin by the 'Senior Man', a student who had been elected by his fellow students to stand as what I suppose was the equivalent of Head Boy at a public school. The college officials and live-in lecturers and postgraduates were together known as the Senior Common Room or SCR, and they had their own separate entrance to the dining room and took all their meals at a 'high table'. All of that was somewhat quaint, but it did help promote and maintain a community atmosphere in the place.

There existed a very sensible arrangement between the various colleges under which any student who knew that he (or she) would not be taking a particular meal could 'sign out', thereby leaving that place to be taken up (at no cost) by anyone who wanted to sign in a friend from another Durham college. It was a really handy system, which encouraged us to socialise with students from other colleges. It was also always possible to book in other visitors in advance, such as family members or friends from outside the university, although payment did have to be made for that.

As I have said, Grey was an all-male college in my time, but just in case you are thinking of feeling sorry for me, don't – because my mates and I certainly did not miss out on female company. Within a radius of about half a mile of our college there were three female-only colleges and a mixed one (later two). Let's just say that I did spend my fair share of time in the female-only ones, St Aidan's College being a particular favourite! Having said that, segregation of the sexes was strictly enforced and it was the job of the college porter (Aidan's porter was named Jack!) to ensure that all visitors had left by 11.00pm, the time of the nightly curfew.

The process of settling in as a 'new boy' was made easier for me by members of the Christian Union. Each college had its own group and the members in Grey made contact with me on the first day. I remember going round to someone's room for coffee that evening and meeting a group of guys for the first time, some of whom later became good friends of mine. One important thing for me about going away to university was that it gave me a chance to pin my colours to the mast as a Christian. That doesn't mean for a moment that my behaviour was always angelic and I would't dare to pretend that. I'm sure there are still plenty of my peers around who could testify concerning some of my antics!

In any event, Durham had a large and thriving Christian Union, known as DICCU (Durham Inter-Collegiate Christian Union). The undergraduate population was about 3,500, of whom approximately 300 were members of DICCU. Additionally, there were separate Methodist and Catholic student societies. Membership of DICCU meant signing up to confirm agreement to a doctrinal position which was distinctly evangelical. We met every Saturday evening in a lecture theatre for worship and prayer, but mainly to hear a visiting speaker. Among these speakers were some of the most famous and inspiring preachers of the day, including men now known by countless Christians, such as John Stott, David Watson and Michael Green. After the meeting, many of the students present would disperse to coffee parties in different colleges around the city, and the speaker would often attend one of those. These socials were a great way to meet other Christians, and many deep friendships, and some long-term relationships, were formed as a result.

One speaker at a DICCU meeting was a solicitor from Manchester, a man called Val Grieve. I started chatting to him at a coffee party afterwards and discovered that his wife was a distant relative of my dad's, from the Tomlinson family in Treales, near Kirkham. Would you believe it? Our paths were to cross again in 1976 when I joined Napthens (then Napthen Renwick & Hosker), because one of the partners was David Sewell, a Christian solicitor six years my senior, who had trained with Val's firm.

I lapped up the teaching at DICCU meetings. As a young Christian I had not had much teaching of any depth until then, but now I was privileged to sit at the feet (literally) of some of the top speakers in the country.

The college CU groups also met weekly, mainly for prayer. I was a regular participant and enjoyed learning a lot from my new friends, especially Peter Stevenson, a softly spoken guy from Northern Ireland who became probably my best friend during my time in Durham. DICCU received regular requests to provide students to help with Sunday services at churches in various outlying parts of County Durham, so Peter and I went together on a number of such trips, to places such as Tow Law and Esh Winning. (Incidentally, there is a village in Durham with the wonderful name of Pity Me, but sadly we were never invited there.) Peter would usually preach and I would lead the service or perhaps give a children's talk, but I think I did preach at least once. We had no private transport, so we usually travelled by bus. Some of the churches we visited were very large, but with small and dwindling congregations, and there could be up to three such churches in what were villages or small towns. During the nineteenth century, County Durham had experienced a Christian revival, so most of those large churches will have been built around that time. Many of the places we visited had once been thriving coalmining centres, but they had fallen on hard times after the pits had closed. It was clear that both the places and the churches in them had known better times, but the people in the churches were very friendly, warm and welcoming, and I guess they were glad to see us. These adventures were new experiences and good training for me. A fantastic bonus was that we were often treated to a splendid Sunday lunch or afternoon tea with families from the congregations.

DICCU did also sometimes provide students to help at church youth clubs around Durham. With Peter, I volunteered to help out at one in quite a deprived area of Spennymoor near Durham, and what sticks in my memory was the behaviour of the teenagers – it was something of an eye-opener for me. For example, I was very proud of my university scarf, and was dismayed to discover on one occasion at the youth club that someone had removed it from a coat hook and had tried to flush it down the toilet!

Peter and I shared a room in Grey for a term in our second year. He studied geography at Durham, but after graduating he went to a theological college in Oxford for a year, and then on into full-time ministry in the Baptist Church. I visited him in Oxford, mainly because in 1976 Peter was planning to get married and had asked me to be his best man – a great privilege and joy for me. The wedding was in Bolton because his wife Susan (whom he had met at Durham) was the daughter of the vicar of the Anglican church in Smithills, near Bolton. Susan also went into the Baptist ministry and eventually she became the senior pastor of a church in South London with Peter on her staff. Peter also then started work as a lecturer at Spurgeon's College in London.

I did keep in touch with the Stevensons for many years. Once, when my wife Chris and I were on our way south on holiday, we called on Peter and Susan at their home near Solihull (they were ministering at Shirley Baptist Church at the time) so that Chris could meet them for the first time. Inevitably, our lives drifted apart and our contact became limited to exchanging cards at Christmas. However, the process of writing this book stirred memories of Peter, prompting me to catch up with him. I discovered that he is now the Rev. Dr P.K. Stevenson, and that in 2011 he was appointed Principal of South Wales Baptist College in Cardiff. We exchanged e-mails and I am determined to meet up with Peter and Susan again.

While in Durham, I did become involved in the local community, as a result of becoming a regular member of the congregation at St Nicholas Church (St Nic's) in the Market Place. It was the traditional evangelical anglican church in Durham and I felt very much at home at St Nic's, but the main reason I decided to get involved there was that they had a Pathfinder group, and I had got to know the then curate of the church, Pete Bye, when he and I were both helping on one of the summer camps at Sandsend. He was still at St Nic's when I went up to Durham, and in fact I had been able to visit him and his wife when I went to Durham for my interviews.

I volunteered to help with the Pathfinder group at St Nic's and made the weekly trek to the far side of the city (on foot) to help out at the meetings at the church's youth centre. It was fun being involved and I felt that I was at least contributing something to the life of the church. One slightly disconcerting matter, however, was that one of the female leaders took a bit of a shine to me. That felt uncomfortable for me because she was some years older than me and I didn't return the interest. She used to offer me a lift back to college after the youth meetings on a mid-week evening, but first she would also take me back to her parents' home for supper, where I enjoyed the luxury of watching *Colditz* on television in the comfort of a domestic lounge rather than in a communal TV lounge back at Grey!

That leads me on nicely to the issue of female relationships at Durham.

So far as romance is concerned, many people naturally meet their life partner at university, but that didn't happen to me. I expect that was a good thing, contributing to my ability to enjoy the full spectrum of life as an undergraduate without the added complications or emotional rollercoaster of relationships. I didn't plan it that way, but as I have hinted already, for at least the first year or so I was still hoping that something might come of a previous relationship at home, naive romantic that I was! What it did mean was that although I had plenty of female friends during my time at Durham I didn't have designs on any of them (for the most part – and even those that slightly interested me came to nothing). This made relationships with all my friends so much easier. One of the exciting events, for example, was that every college held a ball every term, making three dances per year. Two of these were informal balls (glorified discos really, but sometimes fancy-dress affairs), but the other was a formal ball, black tie and all that. These would include a formal dinner, and often a very good live band. I remember that for the 'Grey Ball' one year the college had booked an up-and-coming band by the name of Shakin' Stevens and the Sunsets, no less. We definitely danced on the tables that night!

The deal for the college balls was that you had to take a partner, as tickets were sold as doubles. Everyone understood this and I enjoyed escorting several platonic female friends to such events, or going as a guest of such friends to quite a few others. In fact I think that in one eight-week summer term I escorted nine different young ladies. Happy days indeed, and I still have some photos to prove it!

I did begin to form one romantic attachment towards the end of my time in Durham. There were two very nice young ladies who were good friends and both members of the CU, Fiona and

Dot. Fiona was blonde and pretty, very Scottish and also a good singer. A few of us once went to listen to her in the recording studio in the music department on Palace Green. She and Dot also invited some of us to a Burns Night Supper in their teacher training college, St Hild's, but it was Dot I really fancied. I didn't go out with her before I left Durham, but she was in the year below me, so I returned the following year to look her up and I kept in touch after that. Things progressed from there, but it must have been a year or two later because I remember driving up to see her at her home in Sunderland in my first car, which I didn't own until around the time I qualified, in 1978. I stayed with her family and went to their church with them. Dot also came over to Preston. One year I took her to a New Year's Eve Ball at the rugby club, and we also had a great day out in the Lake District – again, I still have the photos.

One funny episode when I was seeing Dot was at a rugby match. I was playing for Preston Grasshoppers first team at the time, but I was out injured. The team were playing away at Westoe one Saturday and the club officials were puzzled when I asked if I could travel with them on the team coach, because it wasn't usual for guys who weren't playing to do that. However, Westoe is in South Shields, which is only a few miles from Sunderland, and all was revealed when I stepped off the team coach to be greeted by this gorgeous local girl!

Perhaps inevitably, things began to get serious between Dot and myself, or rather we both realised that they would have done if we had carried on seeing each other. We talked about it and then we made the mutual decision to leave it at that and to stop seeing each other.

Going back to my pre-Dot days as an unattached student at Durham, I often attended the regular discos which were held in the students' union building, Dunelm House. We would dance the night away to music by The Rolling Stones, or The Who and the like, but The Beatles were always my favourites. I also remember that some of my more fearsome-looking mates from the university rugby teams (Bobby Anderson springs to mind) would make good money acting as bouncers at such functions, and that there was rarely any trouble when they were on duty.

My friends at Durham were not just members of the CU. I had a good circle of friends in Grey, including guys like Dave Sibbit, John Parkin and Pete Woodward, and in the law department I had mates like Andy Green, Charlie McKenna and Kuba Strycharczyk, with whom I sometimes played football in the inter-departmental five-a-side league.

Life at Durham wasn't all about the Christian Union, sport, or my social life, because I did do some serious studying as well. I worked very hard, as it turned out harder than I really needed to. I think we received about seven hours of lectures each week, plus one tutorial. There were only thirty-five of us on the Honours Law course, so the tutorials were held in small groups and the standard of teaching was very high. However, I decided that I would normally work a nine-to-five day, researching or writing essays in the university library on Palace Green between lectures and tutorials (remember, there was no internet in those days). I didn't normally work on Wednesday afternoons, because I was usually playing rugby then, that is, during the autumn and the spring terms. I occasionally studied in my room on Saturday mornings, but I had resolved from my first week at university that I would not do any academic work on Sundays, because I wanted it to be a day of rest and worship. I stuck to that, even on the odd occasion when I had an exam on the Monday morning, and I'm really glad that I did. I went to church on Sunday mornings and most Sunday evenings as well. I also went out on trips, especially in the summer term. My friend Dave Sibbit actually owned a Morris

Minor 1000, so we were able to visit places like Whitley Bay, the beautiful beaches of Northumberland, or High Force Waterfall in Upper Teesdale.

Initially, my studies at Durham came as a bit of a shock to me. I did enjoy them, but from being a big fish in a small pond at KGS I soon realised that I was an average student in the law faculty. I was certainly not an academic high-flyer, neither was I struggling, but I should have realised early on that I was never going to get a first, and that even a 2:1 was going to be beyond me. We had four final exams at the end of year two, and four more at the end of year three, with a dissertation to do over the summer in between. I did get a 2:1 for my dissertation (almost a first apparently) but when I got four 2:2s in my second year I should have worked out that I would need to get at least four 2:1s in my third-year exams to have any chance of achieving a 2:1 overall. Realistically, that was never going to happen, but like the keen (naive) young lad I was, I continued to 'graft' as hard as I could. In the end I got another four 2:2s, and it was only later that it dawned on me that I could have worked at least ten percent less hard and still got the same result. Doh! By the way, I have since joked to anyone who has cared to listen (and some that haven't) that a 2:2 from Durham is just as good as a 2:1 from most other universities.

I did have some particularly good lecturers. I can't remember all of their names, but Colin Munro, who lectured in constitutional law and supervised my dissertation, comes to mind. Colin Warbrick was another excellent tutor; and I was lectured in criminal law by Leo Blair, a barrister and part-time lecturer, and incidentally the father of Tony Blair, later to become Prime Minister.

I had no means of transport (not even a bike – why didn't I think of that?) so I walked everywhere in Durham. That didn't bother me at all because Durham is a fairly compact city. It was about a twenty-minute walk from Grey down to the law department,

My graduation – July 1975.

which was on North Bailey, near to the castle and the cathedral, and backing onto Palace Green which lies between them. The main shops and St Nic's were also close by. I would often take the scenic route, down a path which led through woodland on the banks which slope down to the river, and over the beautiful three-arched stone bridge known as Prebends Bridge which led onto the Bailey. It was also on that part of the river that some of my friends and I tried punting, trailing the obligatory bottle of wine in the water behind us. The grassy area of river bank near Prebends was a favourite spot for combining sunbathing and revision when summer exams were approaching. It was all very pleasant, especially on a lovely summer's day, but it was when I was walking back to Grey late one winter's night that I gained my most enduring memory of Durham. Allow me to explain...

I had been to a party on the peninsula and was walking home along the Bailey towards Prebends in the early hours of the morning. It was a very calm, still night and there was deep, fresh snow on the ground. It had been very cold for the previous week or two and the river was frozen hard, to quite some depth, affecting the water flowing over the weir just downstream from Prebends and slowing it to a trickle.

I was on my own. There was not another soul to be seen. The street was deserted. The soft snow deadened every other sound which might have reached my ears and all I could hear was the sound of my own footsteps in the snow... crunch, crunch, crunch. It felt exhilarating. It was one of those good-to-be-alive moments... but then I thought I heard something. What was it? At first, I was sure I could hear music coming from the direction of the river, beautiful, lilting piano music. *No, surely not*, I thought, *I must be hearing things*, but it continued and yes, it definitely was a piano, but where was it? I was really intrigued now and had to find out who was creating this wonderful sound in the dead of the night.

Within a few minutes I had reached the river. I made my way to the middle of the bridge and leaned over the parapet, looking upstream. There, in the middle of the river, on six inches of snow, on top of six inches of ice, stood an upright piano. With his back to me, resplendent in full tail-coat, was the pianist, still playing away, oblivious to my presence. I stayed a while, silent, absorbed, thrilled. Then I moved on, still alone and still in wonder. Had I dreamed all of this? No, I definitely hadn't.

It was absolutely wonderful and that, my friends, is what I call style.

Where was I? Oh, yes, speaking of transport, my usual mode

of transport at each end of term was bus, and what a beautiful journey it was! I would send my main belongings in a trunk by train (to be collected from the porter's office at college) but I would travel on the daily coach service which ran between Blackpool and Newcastle, boarding at Garstang (at the bus station, which still existed then). How strange to think that many years later I would be managing a branch office there. Incidentally, I still have the trunk, but now it hides in the loft (stuffed with our Christmas decorations) for eleven months of the year.

The journey took half a day, as the bus trundled through some beautiful countryside and a series of old-fashioned towns and villages. From Lancaster, it proceeded up the Lune Valley to Kirkby Lonsdale, then on to Sedbergh at the western end of the Yorkshire Dales, then to Kirkby Stephen at the far eastern end of what is now part of Cumbria but was then Westmorland, where the bus would stop long enough for everyone on board to buy lunch in a café. After that, we joined the A66 at Brough, went over the Pennines to Bowes, on to Barnard Castle, Bishop Auckland, Spennymoor and finally Durham. It's still a lovely route to follow, although several bypasses have cut the journey time, so it is faster than in those long, lost days.

My 21st birthday fell a few months before I left Durham, so with the agreement of my parents I threw a splendid fancy-dress birthday party at the farm during the Easter vacation of 1975. The theme was 'Stars of the Silver Screen' and everyone who came joined in the spirit of the occasion, dressing up as a whole host of different movie stars or characters. There was Charlie Chaplin, Cleopatra, Frankenstein's Monster and cowboys various (two of whom staged an impromptu gunfight), and countless others. It was a hugely enjoyable time. One of the best things about it was that several of my university friends made the effort to be there, as did some old school friends and friends from home, so it was

a great mix of folk. Andy Green, one of my mates from Durham, arrived in full costume as a Roman centurion, complete with wooden shield and sword; having hitched a lift from the Midlands he had then walked the two miles or so from the motorway to the farm! I have some great photos of the party. I just wish I could remember the names of all the people in them!

I am sad to admit that I have lost touch with just about all my university friends, but I suppose that that is not surprising because it is forty years since we were there. I have had some contact with Andy Green and his wife Julie (née Mohammed), whom he met at Durham and who came to my 21st party dressed as one of two Cleopatras. Andy was from Solihull and like me he was a grammar school lad. He was also average academically and, like me, a keen sportsman (as well as the aforementioned five-a-side football we also played rugby together in the Grey College team). He was a very likeable chap and a real 'people person' who was always likely to do well in life. It turned out that way and Andy went on to become one of the leading lights in DWF, now one of the largest law firms in the North West of England.

By way of contrast, there were a couple of people on the Honours Law degree course in my year at Durham who were academically brilliant, but who simply couldn't relate to others on anything like a normal level. One guy in particular gave every reason to believe that he would never become anything other than an academic lawyer, or perhaps a chancery barrister. I have no idea what happened to him, and he may have proved me completely wrong, but I realised at an early stage that if I was going to have any chance of achieving something as a solicitor I would have to be able to relate well to my clients. Whether or not I have managed that at all is of course for others to judge.

My last three weeks or so at Durham, after my finals were done, were a whirlwind of parties and picnics, champagne breakfasts (well, only one) and farewells. It was great to be able to relax and enjoy a wonderful place with some great friends, but all too soon it was over. One American chap in Grey (whose name I can't remember) said to me on the day we were leaving, 'Bye, Geoff, have a great life!', which summed up my feelings at the time.

The years at Durham were truly some of the best years of my life and I have shared with you many happy memories. Of course it was sad to leave, but the time had come for me to move on to the next stage of life. On to law college.

CHAPTER FOUR

A GOOD IDEA
AT THE TIME
Becoming a Solicitor

Whenever I have been asked why I chose a career in the law I have usually replied that 'it seemed like a good idea at the time'. I realise that sounds rather negative, but as it turned out, life as a solicitor has been good to me. The point I am making is that I never set out with a definite plan to become a lawyer, or even to study law in the first place. All those years ago, my school history teacher suggested that law would be a suitable subject for me to study at university and the advice was good, because it turned out that he was right. I enjoyed the subject, finding it both interesting and challenging, but the main thing was that it held no terrors for me. I realised that it was within my capabilities and that is what encouraged me to continue beyond my degree.

If I was going to try to go on to become a practising lawyer, that decision had to be made part-way through my degree course, because applications for a place on a course leading to professional examinations had to be made about a year in advance, which meant before the end of my second year at university. At some

71

stage before then I had decided that I might as well try for one of the legal professions, but the question was which one: solicitor or barrister?

For those who don't know, there are two main branches of the legal profession in England and Wales, those of solicitor and barrister. Barristers specialise in courtroom advocacy (representing clients in court), but they also draft legal pleadings and give expert legal opinions. Solicitors have more direct contact with clients and many do transactional-type work for them (such as conveyancing). Some solicitors do engage in advocacy, but that is essentially in the lower courts. For the most part barristers receive their instructions from solicitors, rather than directly from clients.

The decision was easy for me, because I just didn't see myself as an advocate, so I didn't fancy becoming a barrister. I did have to undertake some advocacy during my time as a trainee solicitor ('articled clerk' in those days) and as a recently qualified solicitor, appearing in the Magistrates' Court and once or twice in the County Court, and those experiences confirmed that advocacy was not for me. That may sound slightly strange to people who know me well, because I've never found it difficult to stand up and speak in public. I wouldn't say that I have never been nervous, but it has never really bothered me. Chris, my wife, would say that it's because I'm a show-off by nature! The basic rule is to prepare thoroughly, to know what you are trying to achieve and to have a plan of what you will actually say towards that end. You also have to be prepared to be flexible and to adapt what you are saying if things change in some way, even if that happens part-way through your address. I have rarely followed a detailed script and certainly not word for word and I tend to ad-lib quite a bit within a basic framework, or I simply follow a list of bullet points. Obviously, the more familiar you are with the subject matter, the easier that becomes.

There have been occasions when I have had to speak at short notice. A couple of years ago I gave an after-dinner speech to a farmers' club with only eight hours' notice (because the speaker who had been booked was in hospital), but that didn't particularly worry me and I think it went well enough. I realise that many people would find having to say *anything* in public a terrifying prospect, but that's not me and it is a skill for which I am thankful.

One aspect of court work which I definitely did not like was the huge amount of time which was wasted waiting for my case to start. That bored me and I found it very frustrating. When I was an articled clerk I would be sent to the Crown Court to sit behind the barrister representing our client, and that entailed much time doing nothing.

Court work was not going to be for me then. This was the major reason why I decided to qualify as a solicitor and not as a barrister. The system has changed (for the better) since my time, but in order to qualify as a solicitor then, it was necessary to pass the Law Society's part 1 and part 2 exams. A qualifying law degree gave exemption from part 1, so with my law degree from Durham I just had to pass the part 2 exams and then complete two years working for a firm of solicitors as an articled clerk.

At that time only a few institutions provided courses leading to the part 2 exams. There were a few polytechnics doing them, but the best bet was The College of Law, and as they had a college near Chester, that was the one to which I applied. I still had no money, but succeeded in securing a discretionary grant from Lancashire County Council.

Chester appealed for several reasons, and being close enough to home was one of them. Also it's a small and historic city (like Durham), and it's an attractive place to live. I managed to find a bedsit which was adequate, but still pretty depressing. I had never previously lived completely on my own and it was also the first time I had to cook for myself. I was no expert at that, but I got by and I began to enjoy shopping for food and preparing meals – there were no 'ready meals' then – which was a good thing, because learning to cook at least the basics is something which has stayed with me to this day, and which I enjoy.

I had (at last) had the good sense to purchase a second-hand bike, from a friend at home. My bedsit was situated the other side of Chester from the College of Law, which was in the village of Christleton, so I enjoyed the daily cycle ride of three or four miles each way; it offered both daily exercise and time to think.

A nightmare! There is no other word to describe the course. It consisted of six subjects, arranged so that we 'studied' one a month for six months, with exams on all six at the end. There were no tutorials. The lectures were ninety minutes long and basically recited parrot-fashion. In order to pass the exams it was necessary to memorise what was 'taught', virtually word for word. Fortunately for me, some of the subjects were ones which I had covered on my degree course, and I was again helped by the fact that I have always been blessed with a good memory – until now, at least!

At the start of the course we were told that in order to appear in the pass list we must pass a minimum of three subjects at one sitting. In other words, if you passed in less than three of the six subjects you would have to sit all six exams again. We were given the statistics that they expected one third of us would pass all six exams, another third would appear in the pass list, and the rest would fail. Remember, we were all either law graduates or non-law graduates who had already passed the part 1 exams.

I was determined to pass all six exams at once because I certainly didn't want to have to re-do any of that wretched course. The rest of my life (apart from rugby) would have to go on hold. It was only for six months, I reasoned, and I was sure I could put up with that. Nowadays the training process for solicitors is immeasurably better, thank goodness. The Legal Practice Course lasts a full academic year and includes much more practical teaching than the purely academic study of the old system.

The College of Law at Chester did have a mid-week rugby team, organised by a Welsh lecturer by the name of Dai Jones, no less. On my first day in the college I spotted a notice inviting any rugby-playing students to indicate if they were interested in playing for the team and of course my name was the first on the list! As it turned out, there were some very good players at the college, including a guy from Wigan who had played for the full Lancashire team (which was quite something then), and although I wasn't first choice I did still get to play in a number of games and I enjoyed every minute of it.

I had also decided that I would play for Chester Rugby Club, so I ventured down there and made myself available. I played a good number of games, mainly for the third team, and again I found it a welcome break from my mind-numbingly boring college work. I also managed to train there one evening most weeks, riding the two or three miles there and back on my trusty bike.

On Sundays I attended All Saints Church in Hoole, an evangelical Anglican church, similar to St Nic's in Durham. That and playing rugby definitely did help to keep me sane during my six months in Chester. Otherwise it was in fact a pretty lonely existence.

There was a happy ending, as I passed all six exams at one sitting. I sat the exams in a depressing hall (which was quite apt really) somewhere near the Anglican cathedral in Liverpool. It was a huge brick building and there must have been holes somewhere in the roof, because there were pigeons flying around inside while my fellow candidates and I were writing away! The exams were spread over a few days, because I also remember that an old school friend who was working in Liverpool at the time, Hugh Metcalf, kindly invited me to stay at his parents' home on the Wirral. That was a tremendous help, because having to travel back and forth between Preston and Liverpool every day would have made for even more stressful days. As it was, I borrowed my dad's van from the farm and drove to Hugh's house, making my way to and from the Wirral (through one of the Mersey tunnels) at each end of the exam days.

When the exams were over and I was driving back to Preston I thought that I had never felt so tired in my life, but I was also delighted that it was all over – provided I passed of course!

Fortunately, I had two or three weeks free before I was due to start work the following month (March 1976) as an articled clerk with Napthen Renwick & Hosker, now known as Napthens, the firm where I have spent my entire career. I took the opportunity to get some rest at home, but I also spent a day or two in Durham, looking up old friends at the university. I had worked out that there might just be a chance for me to get a game of rugby while I was there. Grey College played their games on Wednesday afternoons, so I timed my journey so that I would arrive around lunchtime on a Wednesday. I went straight to the noticeboard in the corridor in the main building where the team lists were always posted, and I was looking at the rugby notices when a voice behind me said, 'Now then, Geoff, what are you doing here? I don't suppose you've got your boots with you, have you?' Of course I had them – I do like it when a plan comes together – and within half an hour I was on my way to Sunderland to play in an away match for my old college team! Brilliant.

The voice belonged to the team captain, with whom I had played in the Grey team the year before. I'm afraid I can't now remember his name (sorry, captain!) but what I do recall about him is that he was from Todmorden on the Lancashire/Yorkshire border and

Exam

that when Local Government reorganisation of counties happened in 1974 (while we were both at Grey), his home was moved from Yorkshire to Lancashire overnight. As you can imagine, he was not a happy bunny!

I returned to Chester in the summer of the same year, 1976. In addition to the six month course and the six exams mentioned above, prospective solicitors had to pass a separate accounts exam, but the course for it could be taken during the student's two years' articles of clerkship and, better still, his or her employers were obliged to allow a month's paid leave for it. So back to Chester I went, but this time I lived in the YMCA for the month. The accommodation was sparse, but it was perfectly adequate, as was the food. The YMCA was in a great location, down near the River Dee in the very heart of the tourist area of Chester. I had my bike – and it was that unforgettably hot summer of 1976. It was one of the hottest on record and it didn't rain for months. This made the daily ride to the college so enjoyable. I remember that for day after day I would ride shirtless (wearing only shorts and trainers) with my shirt slung over the handlebars and one or two textbooks in the basket at the front of my bike. What made that month all the more enjoyable was the fact that the Accounts Course was an absolute doddle!

Another abiding memory of that time was that when I was there that summer, Chester experienced a plague of ladybirds! There were so many of them that they carpeted the trees and the pavements, turning everything around us completely red.

I took the opportunity to do a lot of fitness training on my own during that July in Chester. I was playing for Preston Grasshoppers first team quite regularly at the time, and as I had to miss part of pre-season training I wanted to do everything I could to be as fit as possible when the new season started that September. I would go for long runs alongside the river in the stifling heat that dominated that summer, as well as doing circuit training on my own. I was keen, if nothing else.

I duly started work at Napthen Renwick & Hosker the following month, at 15 Winckley Square, Preston. On reflection, I suppose some might have accused me of having pulled strings to get the job, or of having taken advantage of the old school-tie connection, but it wasn't like that as far as I was concerned. One of the partners was Peter Hosker and it's true that he was an 'Old Boy' of Kirkham Grammar School like me and I think he was probably already a governor of the school by then. In any event, I had applied for articles with his firm some months earlier and, for whatever reason, had been offered a position.

By the time I started I had also been interviewed by another firm in Preston: Harrison Drury & Moorby, and after I had received the offer from NR&H another KGS Old Boy, Bill Molyneux, got in touch to ask if I would be interested in joining his firm, but by then I had actually already decided to accept the offer from Peter Hosker. It was flattering to be wanted though.

Surprisingly for what was quite a small firm (although probably of medium size by the standards of the day, in Preston at least), I was one of *two* articled clerks who started with the firm on the same day. The other was Geoff Seed, the son of a local butcher and property investor who was a good client of the senior partner, Joe Renwick. Geoff was a bright lad, but he was rather disorganised, and it became clear quite soon that he wasn't cut out to be a solicitor in private practice. Sadly, Geoff didn't last the course and he left the firm to finish his articles with another firm elsewhere. He did qualify with that firm, in Barrow-in-Furness I think, and I believe he also practised there briefly, but he eventually returned to the family business, and made a good job of that instead.

At the start, Geoff and I shared an office room at the back

of 15 Winckley Square, in a part of the building which I believe had at one time been stables. We sat at opposite sides of a very large old oak desk, and shared a telephone. My starting wage was £15 per week, or £780 per annum. Believe it or not, I had to pay some income tax out of that, as well as my bus fares to and from the office. I had gone back to live at the farm because I had no other option really, being without money and unable to afford independent living. Four years later, when I was twenty-six years old, I managed to buy a house of my own.

When I had set out on the path towards a career in the law I had realised that, at best, it would take me five and a half years after A-levels to qualify as a solicitor, assuming that I could manage to pass all the exams first time and then secure articles straight away. As it turned out, I was only six weeks past my 24th birthday when I was admitted to the Roll of Solicitors, which was just about the youngest age at which it could be done then. I was proud of that and also very proud that the Master of the Rolls at the time who signed my admission certificate was the great Lord Denning, who is generally recognised by people in the know as having been the greatest English judge of the twentieth century.

Looking back, I do sometimes wish that I could have taken a year out at some stage to go travelling or something, but for reasons which were practical (mainly financial) that was never a possibility for me. Perhaps I'll go travelling when I retire. Now there's an idea – I must tell Chris right away!

When I started work, the law as a profession was very different from what it is now. For example, completions of conveyancing transactions used to be done face to face, in person; or if you didn't go yourself (because the seller's solicitor might be as far away as London), you had to appoint a solicitor local to the seller's solicitor to act as your agent and do it for you (for a fee). If you

My Certificate of Admission to the Roll of Solicitors, signed by Lord Denning.

were acting for the buyer the procedure was that you had to collect a bank draft for the sum required to complete the transaction; you then went by appointment to the office of the seller's solicitor to attend to the formal completion of the transaction. Very few properties were registered at the Land Registry, so the task generally involved first checking that all the correct deeds were being transferred. Most solicitors would have them ready for inspection, with a typed schedule on top of the bundle, but there were some who couldn't be bothered with that sort of courtesy, so it was sometimes necessary to sort through a very large bundle before going any further. If the deeds were in order, the next job was to ensure that the seller's solicitor was handing over a typed and signed solicitor's undertaking (on headed notepaper) to redeem the seller's mortgage loan out of the sale money, to get the lender to sign a vacating receipt on the mortgage deed, and then to forward that deed to our firm – and to do all of those things 'as soon as conveniently possible'.

The final task was to check that the seller's solicitor was also handing over the conveyance or transfer deed in favour of our client, in the form which had already been agreed, and signed by the seller. Only when you were happy that all of these things were correct did you then hand over the bank draft.

If you think that sounds confusing, I had to deal with a completion like that on my very first day at work. I was articled to Peter Hosker, who sent me to do a completion in Leyland. I travelled by bus, and even though it was only a few miles away I had never been to Leyland before. Quite frankly, I didn't have a clue what I was doing, but the seller's solicitor was very kind and somehow I got through it.

The whole process must have taken about half a day, and looking back it now seems very quaint. Nowadays, everything is done electronically or over the phone and in a fraction of the time. That was nearly forty years ago, so I suppose we shouldn't be surprised, but so much has changed since then.

Articles of clerkship didn't involve the external management courses which are part of the current-day training of solicitors. Articles were more like good old-fashioned apprenticeships, but if the requirement to give the apprentice a proper training was actually taken seriously the system could still work very well. I'm sure there must have been plenty of examples of it not working as intended, and that in my day in particular there were still many articled clerks who were viewed by their employers as nothing more than a source of (very) cheap labour.

I was certainly fortunate in that respect, because Peter did give me a very thorough and rigorous training. I tried to follow his good example when, years later, I had trainees myself. As a trainee, I had to report to Peter every day, and initially I had to get his approval to drafts of any letters or deeds which I had prepared. I had to justify whatever I was proposing, or the position I was suggesting we should take on any particular issue, which is exactly how it should have been. Peter was quite a hard taskmaster, but an effective teacher.

The result of that was that I learned a lot in those two years, and in terms of what it would mean to be a solicitor in the world of private practice that was inevitably far more than anything I had learned at either university or law college. This was about learning the job in practice rather than the law in theory, but it was only the beginning and I still had much more to learn after I had qualified – a process which has continued to this day. I'm sure I made mistakes during my time as an articled clerk, and plenty of them – but I did learn from them, and I'm sure that I grew in confidence, even if that was sometimes as a result of being thrown in at the deep end.

In any event, at the end of my articles (which seemed to come very quickly) I was offered a job as a solicitor with the firm, which I was delighted to accept. I can't remember my starting salary. I know it wasn't much, but at least I was on the ladder.

Chapter Five

STILL LEARNING
(AFTER ALL THESE YEARS)
My career in the law

As my long professional career nears its end, you might be forgiven for thinking that there will be nothing new for me to learn in that closing period, but that is not true at all. The truth is that I am still learning even now, and I expect that to continue until my very last day in the office (which, as I review this manuscript in October 2013, is now only a matter of months away).

I am not thinking about Continuing Professional Development (CPD), the compulsory hours of training which every solicitor has to undergo every year in order to be able to renew his or her Practising Certificate. I do that of course, although to be truthful some of it is of very limited use. Nor do I mean that as office technology continues to develop there always seems to be a new aspect to try to master (sorry, I mean – *learn how to use*); nor am I referring to the fact that I also have to learn and adapt to the occasional changes in the law affecting my clients.

What I want to tell you is that being a solicitor is fundamentally about dealing with *people*, helping them through their problems, their projects, even their pain sometimes, and I for one will never stop learning about people. They still frustrate me sometimes, bring me joy occasionally, and even surprise me every now and then (though not as much as they did when I was younger). The old saying *'There's nowt so queer as folk'* is still so very true.

If ever I had dared begin to think I knew everything about the people I try to serve, that would have been the time to retire there and then, but I'm pleased to say that it never actually happened.

The early years in Preston

For a while after I qualified I didn't specialise at all, which I think was probably the norm. Newly qualified solicitors were encouraged to do a bit of everything. In any event, I found myself doing work as diverse as residential conveyancing, commercial property, accident claims, Magistrates' Court work (including liquor-licensing) and even divorce.

In the course of an initial interview with a client around that time, I was presented with an opportunity which I realised even then would probably never again come my way in the course of my entire career. The client had been summonsed for a routine motoring offence, but it soon became clear that he had a very bad driving record and his licence was already fully loaded with penalty points. The client told me all this and then asked me, 'What's your advice then?' I thought for a moment, looked him straight in the eye and replied, 'Buy a bike!' To his credit the client did laugh, and he didn't disagree with what I had suggested.

I must have done a few things right during the next couple of years because in 1980 the partners offered me a salaried partnership. That was quite something, because I had been qualified for only about two years. I think it was for an initial fixed term of three years, to be followed by an option to buy into full equity (the right to an equal share of profits) by instalments over five years. I was delighted to accept, of course, even though it meant that I would have to borrow the substantial amount of capital which I was being asked to pay to the other partners over the next few years, because it would clearly be a good investment in the long run. I did ask my dad if he could help me out, but he simply wasn't able to do that, so I ended up going to the firm's bank.

For a few years after that things were still tight financially and I had to budget very carefully, especially when I bought the three-bedroomed terraced house that I mentioned earlier. I paid about £8,000 for it, which was a lot of money then, or at least it was to me. I had to stretch myself to afford the loan repayments, but I was happy to do it, because for some time I had been more than ready to leave home. Incidentally, for several years to come I returned to the farm for Sunday lunch most weeks. I took in student lodgers to help me pay my bills, and one year I had two lodgers at the same time, so during term time I rarely had the place to myself.

The house was a Victorian terraced property with large rooms and high ceilings, situated in Fulwood, Preston. I lived there for about four years, including the first six months after my wife Chris and I got married in December 1983. Initially, I would travel to the office in Preston by bus, although I did own a car by then. I remember walking the two miles or so into the office one winter's day when the snow was so deep that the buses had stopped running.

My first car was an Opel Kadett. It was quite large and roomy, but it was very slow. When things got a bit easier I splashed out on a sports car, a Mark 3 Triumph Spitfire convertible. That sounds extravagant, but it had an L registration, so it was already quite old by then. It also had only a 1300cc engine, so it wasn't fast (although it was quite nippy), but it was bright yellow and it certainly looked the part, especially with the roof down on a hot summer day. I had great fun in that car, zooming all over the place. After all, I was a single young man, possibly considered by some to be an eligible bachelor!

So life was good in many ways. By then I was nearing my late twenties and my career was going quite well. I had some good friends and on the surface things were going swimmingly, but there was a major gap in my life. Although I had had one or two girlfriends over the previous few years nothing serious had developed in any of my relationships, and I was beginning to think that I might never marry. I certainly didn't expect that when I was 28 I would meet and fall in love with a 35-year-old divorcee with a four-year-old son and marry her within ten months!

People who know my wife will probably not be surprised to learn that I heard her before I first saw her! It was at a meeting in a side room at Fulwood Free Methodist Church, in January 1983. Chris was singing in a group at the front of the room, but the room was crowded with people, many of them standing, and I was at the back, so I couldn't see any of the singing group.

I heard a wonderful soaring soprano voice and thought to myself, *Who is THAT, singing like an angel?*

I shuffled through the crowd to a better vantage point, and when I caught a glimpse of Chris for the very first time I thought, *And she's not bad-looking either!*

My interest aroused, I made discreet enquiries over the next few days and was pleased to discover that this intriguing, attractive blonde lady was 'available', albeit that she was divorced and had a four-year-old son, Dan. That didn't deter me and I soon found myself 'hanging around' whenever I saw Chris at church over the next few weeks. I found out where she lived and plucked up the courage to go round to her bungalow one evening to ask her out on a date. I had worked out that I would need to invite her to something specific, and that it would have to be something which she might find of interest. At that time I had already been to one or two concerts by the Royal Liverpool Philharmonic Orchestra at Preston Guild Hall, and as it happened another one was due to take place shortly. That seemed ideal so I asked Chris to accompany me, and she agreed!

Incidentally, Chris told me later that after I had first met her parents, soon after our first 'date', her mum had said that I seemed a nice young man and that she thought I was quite handsome. Chris told me that she replied that she knew that her mother was so keen for Chris to meet someone else that she would have said that even if I had had one eye in the middle of my forehead!

Because of the church background in which Chris had grown up she was very sensitive about having been divorced, so we agreed early on in our relationship that, initially at least, we would not tell anyone that we were going out together, and that we would not sit together at church or even be seen talking to each other if we could avoid it. That seemed to work, in the sense that very few people knew that we were becoming 'an item', so to speak. However, it did emerge later that Eva Walton, the wife of the then senior pastor of the church, had worked out very quickly what was going on!

I actually proposed to Chris in the kitchen of her bungalow, while one of her friends was in the lounge! I was thrilled to bits when she said yes. Even then, however, Chris didn't want a fuss, so she didn't have an engagement ring, and we had a very quiet wedding. It was at our church, where we had met, but it was at 10.30 on a cold Monday morning (there was snow on the ground) in December of the same year, on 12th December 1983 in fact. Our guests were limited to immediate family and a few very close friends.

We had a lovely reception at a local country house hotel, and

Wedding, 12 December 1983 – a Happy day!

by about 2.00pm. we were in a taxi to Manchester airport en route to our honeymoon in Tenerife. Dan, who was five by then, stayed with Chris's parents, Les and Grace Seddon, while we were away, but he didn't seem to be bothered, and even as we were being driven away from the reception his attention was focused on the new *Star Wars* light-sabre toy he had just been given!

It was lovely for me to arrive home the day before Christmas Eve, just in time to spend my first ever Christmas with my instant new family; and the following Christmas was also very special for the three of us, because by then our son Andy had come along. Andrew Ralph Tomlinson, a brother for Dan, was born on 3rd December 1984.

Those were very happy days indeed, but the miraculous thing is the fact that Chris has managed to put up with me ever since!

So far as work was concerned it must have been around that time that I made a conscious decision to try to build up the farming side of the practice, and in due course to specialise in agricultural

My lovely wife, Chris, 25 years later, on our silver wedding holiday in New Zealand.

law. The firm already had a reasonable number of farming clients and because of my farming background I tended to be invited to act for them. Some of them knew me, or my family, and soon increasing numbers were beginning to come to the firm because of me, or perhaps initially because of my farming background.

The catalyst for my decision to specialise was an approach from the NFU (National Farmers' Union), or rather from an NFU official called Steve Heaton. He later became North West Regional Director, but at that time the NFU was organised on a county basis and he was the Lancashire Secretary, based at an office in Preston. The NFU in the county already used a firm of solicitors to whom they referred legal work, but Steve wasn't entirely happy with the quality of the service they were providing, and he wanted to know if we as a firm would be interested in going onto an informal panel with them. Naturally, we were interested, and Peter Hosker realised that it was a project for me. As it turned out, one of the partners in that firm was subsequently discovered to have been stealing money from clients, and he was struck off the Roll of Solicitors and sent to prison. That turn of events enabled us to take a lot of business from them and that was really the start of Napthens' dedicated agricultural law service.

I remember meeting Steve with Peter and realising that I was effectively being given an opportunity to create a niche for myself. It was also a chance to prove myself to the other partners because in truth I had been bumbling along until then doing nothing in particular, and they weren't completely convinced that I was bringing in enough by way of fee income. With the benefit of hindsight I think they had some justification.

When I joined Napthens there were four partners. Joe Renwick qualified in the 1930s and until the 1950s was in partnership with Edwin Napthen, the man who had actually founded the firm. Joe was a very intelligent man, but understandably he was rather 'old school'. He was the senior partner and I remember that when we had partners' meetings he would write the minutes by hand into a diary. Peter Hosker had joined in the sixties from a Manchester firm as an ambitious young commercial solicitor. David Renwick was Joe's son (so he wouldn't have had to buy into the business) and he did conveyancing and probate the old way. Finally, there was David Sewell who had joined only a few years before me, also from a Manchester firm. He was a litigator then, but later in his career he became a corporate lawyer and a charity law specialist.

It took me a good number of years to build up my reputation as an agricultural solicitor, but from my point of view at least I now had something at which to aim. I began to speak at farmers' meetings and then seminars. I also began to build relationships with other rural professionals, such as land agents, specialist agricultural accountants and agricultural bank managers, and gradually managed to build up the quantity of work coming in.

We soon became the only solicitors having work referred to us by the NFU in Lancashire.

The Garstang years

The next significant move for me, which also led to a growth in the volume of instructions from farmers, resulted from my first move away from our main office in Preston. The firm as a whole had grown steadily and we had reached the point at which we had outgrown our accommodation at 15 Winckley Square. We decided to buy a much larger office building at 7 Winckley Square (which remains the firm's head office to this day), but before that deal had been completed we began talks for a merger with Houghton, Craven & Dickson, an old established Preston firm who were of a similar size to us and who had office premises around the corner in Winckley Street. Most of their partners had a business outlook similar to ours, and everyone realised that we shared a lot of common ground and that obvious synergies ought to result from a merger. It duly went ahead and overnight we became a fifteen-partner firm, which was very large for a firm of solicitors in Preston at that time.

The merger was not without its issues, however. The first one, perhaps inevitably, was the question of what should be the name of the enlarged business. A compromise was agreed and we settled on 'Napthen Houghton Craven', although we reverted to 'Napthens' after a few years, and that has remained the name of the firm ever since, subject only to the fact that we became a limited liability partnership a few years ago, which changed the legal title to 'Napthens llp'.

The other immediate problem resulting from the merger was that once again we had an accommodation problem, because our new building at 7 Winckley Square was not big enough to accommodate all of the staff who would be staying on from the two firms. The premises in Winckley Street were put on the market, but for a year or two we operated on a split site between Winckley Street and Winckley Square, which was not ideal. The Winckley Street premises were eventually sold for redevelopment (a bar and a pizza restaurant now stand on the majority of the site of the original buildings) and the firm then started to rent part of another building in Winckley Square – number 10. That was better in financial terms, but it still meant that we were operating on a split site. My choice would have been to move out of Winckley Square to larger self-contained offices elsewhere, but (for neither the first nor the last time) I was overruled.

Despite those issues, the merger was fundamentally a big success and it did lead to the practice becoming a much bigger player in the legal market in Preston and beyond.

It is easy to think of the time before all the quality-control systems that are now in place as 'the good old days', when solicitors could trust each other, that is their own partners as well as their competitors. In one sense they were, but the truth is that without file reviews, regular staff appraisals and partner performance reviews it would certainly be very difficult even to survive now, never mind flourish. When I joined Napthens there were probably about fifty firms of solicitors in Preston alone, many of them sole practitioners or two- or three-partner firms in which there can have been little effective supervision of staff and probably no supervision at all of the partners themselves. Within many firms, if not the majority, the partners worked in isolation and if someone had been slacking or worse it is difficult to see how the other partners would have been able to tell.

There were exceptions of course, but many of the local solicitors I came across in the early days, particularly some of the 'old school' guys (there were very few female solicitors), made a good living despite the fact that they were not very good at what they did, and sadly one or two of them were also downright dishonest.

So the profession was viewed with some suspicion and I became aware that my actions and attitudes would always need to stand up to close scrutiny by clients and potential clients. It wasn't a matter of simply trying to look good compared to my competitors, but of doing the right thing, caring about what I did, and being determined to give the very best service possible.

The main implication for me of the merger with Houghton Craven & Dickson was that I was asked to move to Garstang to manage the branch office which that firm had run there for many years (they also had one at Longridge, which the firm retained for many years after the merger, that is until the early retirement of the managing partner there, Steve Wright, following the serious illness and then the untimely death of his wife, Awen). The Garstang office had been run until the merger by David Dickson, who was already semi-retired. He was one of the wider Dickson family, members of which had been involved in that practice for a very long time. He was a lovely chap, a real gentleman in fact, but his way of doing things was understandably old-fashioned and he was far from dynamic.

When the firm asked me to take over leadership of the branch I was glad to do so and I saw it as another opportunity to prove myself. My final progress to full equity in the practice (the right to an equal share of profits) had been held back because the partners in the firm as it was before the merger had intimated to me that they still didn't think I was billing enough in fees and asked me not to exercise the last part of the option which I had been granted earlier. I was really quite annoyed about that stance and briefly considered leaving the firm, but I decided in the end to stay and to try to prove my worth to the business as a whole. The merger and the move to Garstang gave me the opportunity to do precisely that.

Garstang was an ideal environment for me: a friendly market town in the middle of a large farming area, with obvious potential to build the farming side of the practice. In the nine years for which I was at Garstang the turnover of the branch increased fivefold and a large part of that was due to new business from farmers and landowners. However, not all of that growth was purely agricultural law work, and the fact of having an increased presence in the office, and having it manned full-time by a partner in the firm, pulled in more general high-street business, such as residential conveyancing, wills and probate, general litigation and divorce cases; but I also invested a lot of time and effort liaising with other professionals in the area, and potential referrers of business in particular.

The existing staff at the Garstang office were very friendly and helpful. We had a long-serving legal executive, Heather Wood, who did conveyancing and probate work. She doubled up as Registrar of Births and Deaths; and litigation was covered by one of the HC&D partners from Preston, John Woosnam ('Woosie') He was already then spending one day a week at the Garstang office, but the increasing volume of contentious work meant that he soon found himself having to be there for two days most weeks. Later on, we recruited a trainee, Pat Newell, a mature student who had done various jobs before going into the law and who therefore had quite wide life-experience. He was based at the Garstang office and covered much of the litigation work there, under John's supervision. Pat then stayed on with the firm when he qualified, working mainly in agricultural litigation for many years, although he did eventually leave the firm to work elsewhere.

It was during the early years at Garstang in particular that I got to know Woosie well, and he became a real source of help and encouragement to me. If we got time, we invariably wandered down to the Church Inn on market day for a pub lunch and a good old chat, and even the odd game of pool.

John's companionship and support were very helpful to me, because although I enjoyed the autonomy of running my own branch, I sometimes felt isolated and John's input alleviated that.

The support staff at Garstang were a great bunch and we created a happy and effective team. Two very good long-serving secretaries, Margaret Tinsley and Margaret Pinder, were already working there when I moved to Garstang, and initially my then secretary from the Preston office, Joanne McHugh (as she then was), moved with me, but after a couple of years she left, to marry a client! Joanne was a lovely lass and an extremely good secretary. Moira Haycock then joined the firm to become my secretary and she worked for me until we closed the branch in 2000. She also continued with me for a while after I moved back to our Preston office, but she was then offered a job back in Garstang, which was more convenient for her as it was closer to home. Moira was also a very good secretary, but in addition to that she was a real caring soul who would help anyone if she could. She is only a couple of years older than me and we got on very well and became good friends over the time we worked together.

At different periods during my time in Garstang the team was also joined by Marjorie Crossley and Rachel Sumner, but whoever was in the team we had some really good times together. We enjoyed meals out together at Christmas or to celebrate someone's birthday (often accompanied by our spouses), and more than once we all dressed up in Victorian garb to join in the fun at the town's annual Christmas festival on the High Street. For several years we also had our own tent at Garstang's annual agricultural show in early August, which is probably the main event of the year for the town. For many of the years in which we did that, we laid on catering ourselves (for clients and guests) and we all worked very hard together. Those were long days, but great fun too and again, I have the photos to prove it!

I worked very hard during the Garstang years. I remember being so busy one autumn that I had to go into the office on my own for several hours on seven successive Saturdays, just to complete all the paperwork.

Above: With Garstang office staff at our tent at Garstang Show – it must have been a wet one that year.

Below: The Garstang office team, all dressed up ready for the annual Christmas Victorian Festival.

Inevitably, we experienced some sad times when I was at Garstang. The worst day of all, which I will never forget, was when fourteen-year-old Andrew, the younger of Moira's two sons, was killed in a road accident. He was knocked off his bike while doing his morning paper round. We all asked ourselves how you get over something like that and realised at once that the answer is of course that you never do.

Overall, those years were happy ones for me and saw me through from my mid-thirties to my mid-forties. I was working hard, enjoying it and being rewarded well financially, and at home my family was growing.

Why did that period come to an end? The answer is that it was all to do with the NFU.

Relaxing on holiday in Majorca, circa 1986.

NFU Panel – and back to Preston

In 1999 the NFU decided to create a national legal panel, with the service being provided by specialist agricultural solicitors from nine different firms of solicitors, each covering a different part of England or Wales and with the whole thing being backed up by a national call centre. The idea was that NFU members would be encouraged to raise queries of a legal nature with the call centre, rather than with their local group secretary, and the call centre would then refer to the relevant panel firm any matters which they were unable to resolve themselves. Group secretaries were also to be encouraged to direct any such queries to the call centre, rather than sending them to non-panel firms of solicitors or trying to deal with matters themselves. It was also part of the deal that the firms on this panel would be asked to contribute to the costs of establishing and running the call centre.

Firms applying to go on the panel had to undergo a rigorous application process, and those appointed would then be audited by the NFU on an ongoing basis. As we already had a connection with the NFU we were invited to apply for membership of the panel, which we did, but we soon realised that we were probably the smallest of the firms under consideration. Fortunately, there was limited opposition in the North West and we were duly appointed to be the panel firm for Cumbria, as well as Lancashire. Although the panel has changed significantly since then (for example, there are now sixteen firms on it nationally) we have managed to retain our position as the sole panel firm for both Lancashire and Cumbria, and remain one of only a few to have been on the panel ever since 1999.

John Woosnam and I had dealt with the application on behalf of Napthens, and we attended the initial meetings and interviews together, that is after the identity of the members of the initial panel was announced. Those early meetings were quite exciting, if not a little daunting, but we also greatly enjoyed mixing socially with other specialist agricultural solicitors from around the country, some of whom were great characters.

Prior to our appointment Napthens hadn't signed up to any kind of quality assurance scheme, and the NFU had made it clear that it was a condition of our appointment that we would go down that route immediately. We duly did so and that was in effect the beginning of the real modernisation of the practice.

In the lead-up to the creation of the NFU Legal Panel we were told by the man in charge of NFU Services Limited (as it then was), the company running the operation for NFU and NFU Mutual, that all of the firms involved would be bound to have very significant volumes of legal work referred to them, and very substantial additional fee income for each firm was confidently predicted. The figures suggested turned out to be wildly over-optimistic. However, we as a firm decided that we would need to form a dedicated team of agricultural lawyers who would handle the promised flood of new work. At that stage that involved me and some of our litigators (led by Woosie).

With my experience, I was the obvious person to lead that new team, which needed to be based at our main office in Preston because of the numbers of staff who would have to be involved. Taking me out of Garstang meant that we could no longer justify keeping the Garstang branch open. Closing it was not what I wanted but I wasn't in a position to contest the decision, because I was keen for the NFU experiment to succeed, which in the long run, it did.

With the benefit of long hindsight we should have created a dedicated agricultural team at Garstang (using bigger and better premises if necessary). I suggested that at the time, but without sufficient force and, as it happened, we lost some non-agricultural clients from the Garstang area but we did manage to retain most of our farming clients from there.

In any event, I moved back to Preston and the firm rented an extra floor at 10 Winckley Square, for the exclusive use of the new agricultural team. We gained more work from the NFU, but nothing like the amount that had been envisioned. Before long that floor got filled up with general litigation solicitors and a scattering of their work mountain, so the agricultural law team (myself, supported by a couple of litigators and the occasional trainee) transferred to a different part of that building, to free up space for others.

Team expansion – Blackburn, then Penrith

Before we left Garstang the volume of legal work for farmers had grown to the point where there was enough to keep one and a half people busy, but not enough to enable us to justify recruiting an assistant for me, or so I thought. I know now that I should have pushed for help, if only because I was struggling to find enough time to do any kind of business development work.

I had realised early on that the nature of doing legal work for farmers is such that I could complete a single job for a farmer and then not hear from him again for ten years or more, simply because he had felt no need for my services in the intervening period. That taught me that it was vital to be going out and winning new clients all the time, so I have always constantly sought new ways of reaching them, and of bringing my services to their attention. Over a period of several years all that hard work began to bear fruit, and in due course it became the norm for more than a quarter of the annual fees billed to farming clients to have come from clients who were completely new to the firm. That was (and still is) a very healthy statistic, but also a scary one. On the one hand, that kind of growth is difficult to maintain, but on the other hand, once it is achieved consistently significant growth happens when repeat business from existing clients also comes in on top of the new stuff.

We have also always aimed to keep our name in front of farmers as much as possible, partly by being involved in farming events and by putting on different kinds of seminars, but also by sending out regular newsletters (and now e-updates) to farmers and rural professionals and occasionally writing articles for the farming press.

We eventually recruited an assistant for me when I returned to the Preston office, but he struggled with the work and left of his own volition after about eighteen months. The situation seemed desperate, but then I struck lucky. We recruited Andrew Holden from another Preston firm. He had qualified a year before and had been doing residential conveyancing work and some commercial property matters, but he was a local lad with some farming connections and we sensed he had something about him.

I did my best to train Andrew in various areas of law which are specifically agricultural and he attended a number of suitable training courses. He was a fast learner and also proved himself to be good with clients, and hard-working. The outcome is that, some seven years later, Andrew became head of our Rural Business Department (as I had decided to rebrand it before Andrew joined the firm) and therefore my line manager! Andrew has already done very well in that role, since I stepped down from it with effect from 1st April 2012. He has gained the confidence of clients and referrers alike, and it is especially pleasing that Andrew has risen to the challenge of leadership – all with the added bonus that it took the pressure off me. The future of the department is in safe hands.

The rural team also has another gem in Melissa Taylor, who

was recruited as a trainee solicitor in 2009. Originally, we had been planning to take on only one trainee that year, but Melissa's mother, who at that time was an NFU Group Secretary, got in touch and asked if we would consider Melissa. We interviewed her and realised immediately that she would be a very strong candidate to work in a specialised rural law department. She is from a farming family, and was then still living on her dad's dairy farm in the Lune Valley. She was heavily involved in Young Farmers, and she had a very impressive academic record. Taking into account all of those factors, it was an easy decision for us to make, and we offered Melissa a training contract, on the basis that during the first year she would be trained in other departments (litigation, and probate and trusts) and would then spend the whole of her second year in the Rural Business Department, with a view to staying on after qualifying. What a good decision that turned out to be! Melissa got rave reviews from both Litigation and Probate and as soon as she started in Rural we realised what an asset to the team she would become. I realised that we would be mad not to keep Melissa on after she qualified, so I pressed for that very strongly, but there was some uncertainty as to how much non-contentious rural work would become available. On the face of it we would need to keep all three of us busy full time, and although there was obvious potential for Melissa to bring in new clients through her own farming connections, that was unproven.

There was an obvious solution – in that I had already indicated to the firm that I wished to reduce my hours to a three-day working week. I proposed that formally, and it was agreed. I had originally had it in mind to change to a three-day week when I turned 55, but that hadn't worked out.

The new arrangement worked well for me and I had no complaints. It also made the way clear for Melissa to be appointed as an assistant solicitor in the Rural Business Department when she qualified in September 2011. It soon became clear that that had been absolutely the right move for the firm, and the department continued to grow strongly thereafter. Melissa is very pleasant and not at all pushy, but she is also quite prepared to argue her corner and has already stood up to solicitors with vastly more experience than her. Her special talent is her ability to 'think outside the box' and to look beyond the obvious. In short, she will go a long way in the law.

Another significant development for the rural team occurred at the time Melissa qualified. Earlier in 2011 the firm had decided to relocate its existing Blackburn office, following a similar move by the Blackpool office team, which had been completed in May of that year. In both cases the firm was leaving tired old town-centre premises with poor access and inadequate parking in order to move into new or refurbished modern offices on a business park on the outskirts of town. As I have mentioned already, I had long had an issue with the rural team being located in one of the firm's two offices in the city centre of Preston. By this time, the rural team had moved from 10 Winckley Square into number 7 in order to facilitate an internal reorganisation, but it was far from ideal for our farming clients and contacts; farmers in particular had always been reluctant to come into the office. We always made a point of being willing to go 'on farm' whenever that could be justified, but there were some occasions when it was necessary for them to come in to see us. I understood why they were not keen on having to fight their way into the city centre, particularly as access was not ideal and parking at the office was limited.

At that time, I was still head of the department, so when I heard about the proposed Blackburn move I suggested that my team should perhaps relocate there, having first checked with both Andrew and Melissa that they were happy with the idea. They were, and my proposal was accepted by the firm. Our rural team had always ventured away from the office to see clients all over the North West and we knew we would benefit if there was easy access and parking, so we were relieved that the move to Blackburn enabled us to offer that facility for our clients.

It soon became clear that relocating there had been the right decision. It was further to travel to work but it was a stress-free journey, and I for one adapted to it quickly. More importantly, it proved popular with clients and contacts, many of whom were immediately much more willing to visit the office. We joined the existing Blackburn team and during our first year that team grew in number. It was another happy office, with a good team spirit, and the overall performance of the branch was soon on the up and up. However, my time working there lasted only about fifteen months, because a new development for the firm meant that it was soon time for me to move on again.

Napthens has developed significantly over the last five or six years in particular and it is now a major player in the legal market across the North West and beyond. The growth of the Rural Business Department had been more gradual, but significant momentum had been built up and I was sure that the opening of a new Cumbria office in Penrith would aid that process. I agreed to become fully involved with this venture because, although I was already scheduled to retire at the end of March 2014, two weeks after my sixtieth birthday, it was an exciting and challenging new project. I was confident that it would succeed, and hoped it would be a satisfying way for me to conclude my time with Napthens before it became time for me to ride off into the proverbial sunset!

The Cumbria office opened on 2nd January 2013 and the signs quickly became very promising. Rural business provided the catalyst for the move, but the plan was (and is) for the office in Penrith to be developed into a full-service commercial office. I was to be based there for my three days a week and we recruited an excellent local rural solicitor, Alex Sykes. In the Blackburn office Siobhan Turner, who is also very experienced at handling rural property work, joined us as Andrew Holden's assistant and that in turn enabled both Andrew and Melissa to spend time helping at Penrith. Those appointments meant that we had a team of five specialist rural lawyers doing non-contentious work. In addition, there were five or six others who spent some or all of their time on specialist agricultural litigation. So it had become a considerable team, with further appointments likely to follow, particularly in Cumbria.

I was still doing what I had always loved: working with farmers and other like-minded professionals, but just in a different part of the North West.

CHAPTER SIX

WOULD YOU LIKE A BIT OF DINNER?

The most important people: my clients

I first spoke to a farmers' meeting quite early in my career. A client who was connected with the Tenant Farmers Association (I think he was the chairman of the Lancashire Branch) had invited me to speak about agricultural tenancy law. Looking back, my talk, although technically correct, was given more from theory than from experience but it seemed to go down well, perhaps because I made sure that I mentioned my farming background. As I was leaving, the chairman thanked me and said that it was good to have a solicitor who understood farming. I replied that that wasn't quite correct and that what little bit I knew about farming came from having grown up on a small dairy farm, but that I liked to think I knew a bit about farmers themselves.

That is the key point. Farmers are a different breed. They think differently, they express themselves differently and their priorities differ significantly from those of most of the rest of the population. In order to have any chance of success, anyone who deals with farmers in any capacity needs to understand that. Someone from a farming background has a head start in that respect. I knew that I had that, and that I was very fortunate.

It's all about relating to your client, understanding what that client wants, what are his priorities and the particular pressures he faces at any given time. Within farming that can depend a lot on the sector within which he operates, because these things tend to go in cycles and a farming sector which was doing well one year can find itself struggling the next, whether as a result of something as basic as the weather, or perhaps because of political decisions made by others. A solicitor hoping to act for farmers needs to be aware of such trends. I have always said that I have been very fortunate to have acted for clients throughout the North West, because just about every single type of farming is represented here. This includes, for example, some areas in south Lancashire where significant acreages of combinable crops are grown.

That principle applies just as much to solicitors working in other disciplines, or for clients with businesses in other industries. I'm sure many of my colleagues do understand how important it is at least to try to gain a basic understanding of the client's business, what it does, how it works, the challenges it faces and the opportunities it presents. At the very least, it is a good idea to show an interest in the client and in what makes him tick. He will then see that you are interested in him and will hopefully appreciate that you really are on his side.

However, for a large part of my career my profession has structured itself in ways that have suited itself, rather than the people who pay its bills, namely the clients. The client is not the least bit interested in how law firms organise themselves internally, or whether we label ourselves as corporate lawyers or litigators, or whatever it might be. Despite that, it was decided many years ago that we at Napthens would split ourselves internally into a Private Client Division and a Commercial Division. In itself, there was nothing wrong with that and there is no doubt that it helped improve the efficiency of our internal administration and management, but there was always a danger that that sort of thing might influence the way we think about clients. There was also a practical difficulty for me and my team, because I saw myself as a solicitor acting for farmers and landowners, rather than as a commercial or private client lawyer, and that meant that I never really knew whether the Rural Business Department belonged in the Commercial Division or the Private Client Division. Partly because of the title it carries, it was actually placed in the Commercial Division. That was despite the fact that the work often involves advising the farmer and his (or her) family about their private affairs as well as on matters affecting their business, the best example of that being the whole issue of farm succession (of which more later), which necessarily involves the making of wills but also consideration of the whole future of the business.

I could never say that my dealings with clients have been dull. They have intrigued and stimulated me, frustrated and even annoyed me. They have rewarded and delighted, they have made me laugh and have even made me cry, but it has certainly never been dull.

In this chapter I will relate just some of the many things which have happened in the course of my dealings with clients, some of them poignant, some downright hilarious; and I will also explain some of the lessons I learned along the way and principles I established which helped me as my career progressed.

The title of this chapter comes from something which was said to me by a farmer client's wife many years ago, when I was heading up my firm's branch office in Garstang. I had gone to see some clients on their farm near Pilling, together with their accountant. If I mention that he was a chap who liked his food, I think one

111

or two people in that area might be able to work out who it was. Incidentally, I happened to be speaking to him recently and when I mentioned the incident to him he remembered it very well.

In any event, we had concluded our business and it just happened to be about lunchtime ('dinner-time' in Lancashire). The accountant and I were about to leave when the farmer's wife uttered those immortal words: 'Would you like a bit of dinner?' When we both said yes (it really would have been rude to have refused), a 'bit' of dinner turned out to be a hearty feast (three courses!) of real home-cooking. What a treat it was and all the better for not having been expected.

That was not the only such incident; in fact it was one of very many such instances of kindness and hospitality shown to me by clients over the years, often at our very first meeting. It is very 'James Herriot', I know, but when I go to a farmhouse to meet new clients I am still invariably offered a drink of tea or coffee, and more often than not home-made cakes and biscuits. I have enjoyed hearty breakfasts in farmhouse kitchens, as well as lunches. I have been given sacks of potatoes, carrots and cabbages, bags of curly kale and trays of eggs, packs of duck breasts, and all sorts of home produce, all because the good farming folk I was dealing with simply wanted to be hospitable. I understood that, because my mother would have done exactly the same thing. Fundamentally, it's simply because that's the way farming folk are, and who wouldn't want to act for people like that?

One of the funniest things a client ever said to me happened many years ago. This farming couple had already then been clients of mine for a long time, and I had come to regard them as friends as well as clients. The husband had undergone a serious back operation and I remember going to visit him in hospital. A few months later, I was speaking to his wife and asked how he was progressing. She replied that he was fine as long as he didn't

put too much strain on his back, or try to lift heavy weights. I should have left it at that, but oh no, not me. Like the idiot I can be sometimes, I asked her, 'And has he got to chasing you around the bedroom yet?' Without hesitating for even a fraction of a second, she replied, 'Who says he has to chase me?' That put me in my place, didn't it? It cracked me up at the time and still makes me chuckle every time I think of that conversation. I suppose it was just the response I should have expected from the wife of a farmer, and a pedigree Holstein breeder at that!

Something you soon learn if you have dealings with farming families over any length of time is that many of them are related to each other, particularly in certain geographical areas. In the Pilling area of Lancashire, for example, it seems that almost every other person is called Jenkinson, and in Chipping there are plenty of Hardmans. Particular family names are in fact still very common in many villages around the North West of England and a lot of those people will still be involved in farming. There are a number of Tomlinsons in and around the Fylde as well but, as I mentioned in a previous chapter, we were a separate clan from those we regarded as the wealthier ones. On several occasions, especially early on in my career, I discovered about ten minutes into an initial chat with some new clients that they were related to me, even if their name was not Tomlinson.

I learned early in my career that it was always a good idea to establish the antecedents of the other party to a conversation before even hinting at anything even remotely like a derogatory comment about a third party, because they might be related to that person. (So a life lesson: check who you are talking to before you insult anyone!)

Historically, the reason for this phenomenon about surnames is obvious. For centuries, the only form of transport available to most farming families was foot power. Some might have had access to a horse or a donkey, or later on perhaps a bicycle, but few people in country areas would have had much access to any form of motorised transport (and certainly not their own) until towards the middle of the twentieth century. That meant that farming folk didn't travel far beyond their own village, and for some a journey to the nearest town would be a very occasional thing, even a once-in-a-lifetime trip.

My own late brother-in-law, Ray Wilkinson, who died suddenly in 2003 at the age of 56, told me after he had passed his fiftieth birthday that until that point he had never been on a train in his life. Mind you, he did spend just about all of his life in Out Rawcliffe, so that probably had something to do with it! In any event, the lack of available transport until quite recently did mean that village folk tended not to venture too far away from their home area, and that if a farmer's son wanted to find a wife he would probably not go much further than the next village, or even the next farm. Inevitably, that also meant that many locals ended up marrying their own cousins. That in turn might explain why, if you spend any time in the pub in some villages, before long you will notice that many of the local lads bear a striking resemblance to each other.

Even if they are not related to each other, most farmers know a lot about each other and the minutiae of their local rural community (such as who has died, who is struggling financially, who is buying more land – things like that) or even further afield, and occasionally I was made aware that they knew what I had been up to as well! I once went to see some lovely people, clients of mine in the Yorkshire Dales, and was greeted by the comment, 'I believe you were in Ormskirk the other day.' I had been, but I couldn't work out how they knew and I couldn't name the people I had been to see because of client confidentiality. The client then solved the problem for me by explaining that the farmers I had been to see were the family of his daughter's boyfriend, or husband or something like that – I can't remember the details.

The close links within the farming community as a whole, and not just within particular farming families, have worked to my advantage many times over the years. The best source of new work for any business is personal recommendation and I'm pleased to say that many of my clients have been kind enough to recommend me to their friends and neighbours, as well as to their kin. I have made a point of thanking them whenever that has happened, although sometimes I have discovered who passed on my name only as a result of asking the new client why he had chosen to contact me. So another tip for all agricultural lawyers to remember: if you don't know at first why a new client got in touch, remember to ask, so that you can then thank the person who recommended you.

One consequence of knowing and being known by a lot of farmers and their families, as a result of having had a long career, is that when I am out with my wife we do seem to keep bumping into people I know. Actually, to be slightly more precise, I should have said 'people who know *me*', because I must admit that there have been occasions when the farmer and his wife have clearly known me, and I recognised them, but I couldn't remember their names!

We have met clients in all sorts of locations, even when we have been on holiday at the far end of the country. I remember that we were once in the museum at the Royal Worcester factory when we bumped into the couple from the farm which was the nearest one to our house at the time, and which had land running right up to our garden.

As well as dealing with farmers themselves, I have also had encounters with some of their animals, including their dogs. I grew up accustomed to farm animals, particularly cows, so being around them never bothered me and I knew how to behave, but I haven't always been able to say the same about dogs. We always had dogs on our farm, usually mongrels and more often than not pretty useless as working animals. Some of them were daft because they were young, but others were just daft.

One story about a young dog dad used to tell came from the days when we still used to make hay. He had spent the best part of a hot summer day working the hay, driving the tractor (and whichever hay-making machine he was using) round and round the field. The young dog, keen never to be too far away from its master's side, followed him all day long, round and round the field, just a yard or two behind, and it was exhausted by the time the job was done. That wasn't the case for the older dog which dad also had at the time, though. It just sat in the gateway all day and watched!

That reminds me of the story about the young bull and an old bull which were standing together at the top of a field, gazing on a group of heifers at the bottom of the field. The young bull was getting quite excited, and he said to the old bull, 'Let's run down to the bottom of the field and "bull" one of those heifers.' 'No, lad,' said the old bull… 'Let's walk down and bull 'em all!'

I did grow up with a dog of my own, a border collie called Whisky. I don't know why she had that name, but if she was within earshot anywhere on the farm all I had to do was to shout her name at the top of my voice and she would soon appear by my side. It never dawned on me that it must have sounded very strange to any visitors if they heard a little lad shouting 'Whisky!' at the top of his voice. She was one of our better dogs, a good worker and very affectionate. She was apparently the same age as me and I can remember her being at my side, or at least nearby, virtually all of the time when I was at home. She died when I was fourteen. I remember being very sad as we buried her in a quiet corner of the orchard. Growing up with Whisky is still a lovely memory for me, but despite that, I have always been wary of certain kinds of dogs, especially Alsatians (or 'German Shepherds').

When I was about ten I used to go round to play with a friend, Ray Stansfield, who lived in a bungalow next door to Horace Coupe's pig farm, which was only a couple of hundred yards from the end of our farm road. The problem was that Horace had a large and very nasty Alsatian, which roamed free in his yard. Unfortunately, in order to reach Ray's back gate I had to ride my bike through that yard – do you see where this is going? I tried to be brave and even to appear nonchalant, but it didn't work, and I was sure the dog knew that I was scared, which only made things worse. There was a gentle slope down from the road to the far end of the yard, so I used to freewheel down it, while bringing my right leg round behind me, ready to hop off my bike as quickly as I possibly could the very second I had reached safety. Would you believe it? One day, when I was halfway through the manoeuvre, the blessed hound jumped up and bit me on the backside!

A much funnier incident involving a dog happened relatively recently (well, I thought it was funnier, but I guess you are thinking the one I have just recounted might be pretty hard to beat). I had called to see some new clients on a farm which was on a hillside near Rochdale. It was a wet and windy day (as often seems to be the case in that area) and the yard was open and exposed. As I drove into the yard I clocked an evil-looking Alsatian in the yard. Thankfully, it was on a chain, but I still took great care to drive past it very slowly as I advanced through the yard, as far away from it as I could manage. I didn't want to risk upsetting it, but I have to admit that it did look pretty unhappy with life as it was. *Phew*, I thought, *I've succeeded in passing it safely*, as I parked the car beyond its reach… but that was when things started to go wrong.

WOULD YOU LIKE A BIT OF DINNER?

As was my custom, I had placed on the front passenger seat my notes from my initial phone conversation with the clients, a couple of handwritten sheets with their basic details, names and phone number etc. (in case I got lost on the way and had to ring them for directions, although that didn't happen too often). As I opened the car door and started to climb out a strong gust of wind picked up the papers, sucked them out of the door past me, and deposited them onto the surface of the yard, underneath the car. *Great*, I thought, *I'm going to have to get down and retrieve them from under the car.* If only it had been that simple...

Just as I was getting down to see where the papers had landed, another gust picked them up and blew them out from under the car, across the yard, towards the dreaded hound, which by now was pulling against its chain with all its might, straining to get at the intruder who had dared to invade its territory. I now had to move quickly, but two questions immediately flashed into my mind. Would the papers be blown further towards the dog before I could retrieve them, and exactly how long was that chain anyway?

It was becoming a challenge, so I crouched down and inched my way towards the papers, which were clearly in view in the most open and exposed part of the yard, and thereby closer and closer to the dog. Nervously, I stretched out my left hand towards both my prize and my possible nemesis. If it bit off my left hand at least I would survive (I reasoned with myself), and after all I am right-handed. It must have looked like a scene from a Buster Keaton silent movie!

Fortunately, the clients-to-be were still happily ensconced in their warm and cosy farmhouse, not having ventured out into the gale to greet me, despite the fact that the baying of the hound (which would have terrified Sherlock Holmes, never mind me) must surely have alerted them to my arrival by then. I was also

119

pleased that there was no window in the side of the farmhouse which faced that part of the yard through which they might have enjoyed viewing my discomfort (mind you, if there had been, they probably could have boosted their finances quite considerably by selling tickets to all and sundry to come and watch at close quarters what I suspect was not an isolated incident in that yard).

Thankfully, I managed to retrieve the papers and beat a hasty retreat (sorry to disappoint you!) and, doing my best to regain my composure, I made my way to the back door of the farmhouse. The farmer said nothing about his dog, that is until I was about to leave an hour or so later. 'I'd better come out with you,' said he, 'because my dog's in the yard and he can be a bit nasty.' 'Oh, that's all right,' I replied, as I thought, *I wish you'd told me that before I came!*

A final thought about dogs is that one of them did once help to teach me an important lesson. It was quite common when I was young for companies to fly over farms, taking photographs, and then to send a salesman to the farm a week or two later to try to sell the farmer a framed aerial photo of his farm, or at least of part of it. Dad bought a couple of those over the years, and after my parents retired they had pride of place on the walls of their bungalow. One in particular was very revealing. It was summer time and dad and I had been working down the fields. We were walking back to the farmhouse in the late afternoon. I remembered having seen the plane fly over at the time.

When the photograph arrived, dad was clearly visible on it, walking alongside one of our farm buildings (the cow kennels). Within a metre of him was his dog, and at least a few paces behind the dog was, you guessed it, yours truly! If I hadn't already realised it by then, the lesson I learned that day was my position in the pecking order on the farm, that is to say, one below the dog.

In the course of dealing with farmers over so many years I have seen tragedy. I have known of clients losing limbs in farm accidents and some have even lost their lives that way. I have had clients deteriorate into dementia, some even becoming uncontrollably violent towards their immediate family. Some have become mentally ill earlier in life, or have declined into alcoholism.

I suppose all of those things are part of the general human condition, and of course farmers are equally susceptible to whatever life throws at them, but it is a fact that farming as an occupation ranks very highly in the league table of occupations whose members are most likely to commit suicide. Some farmers can be more prone than most to depression (my own grandfather was a sufferer), and that is clearly not helped by the work being an often isolated and lonely existence. Where it is available, family support is vital, but in my view the friendship and sense of common purpose which can be offered by farmers' clubs or discussion groups also have an important role to play. Organisations like RABI and FCN (Farm Community Network, previously Farm Crisis Network) also do vital work, offering practical and moral support where they can, but they need to know where the needs exist and farmers can be very slow to ask for help for themselves.

If you know someone involved in farming who is in need of help, be it a farmer or farmworker, or a member of their families, please do something about it. The first step might be to contact RABI or FCN, both of whom operate in the strictest confidence. Their contact details are printed at the end of this chapter.

I have also witnessed difficult, sometimes tragic, situations arise within farming families after a death, simply because advice was not sought, or the right advice was given but not followed. A simple example is that if a partner in a farming business dies unexpectedly and there is no partnership agreement or life insurance in place, the damage which can result to the business and to the family is obvious. If the deceased partner had a substantial amount of capital in the business and his estate passes to his widow (who may have had nothing to do with the business), it can then be impossible for the surviving partners even to agree terms on which to pay out his estate, never mind raise the money which would be required.

If a farmer dies intestate (that is, without having left a will) and his estate passes automatically to his four children equally between them, and only one of them is involved in the business, how is he or she going to be able to pay out his or her siblings? The answer is almost inevitably that that will simply not be possible, and that the end result will be that the farm will have to be sold.

You would think, wouldn't you, that it should be obvious that even just the simplest form of planning (such as making a will) should be done in cases like that? I'm afraid the reality is still that far too many farmers simply don't prepare for death properly. Some just never get round to it, or do nothing because they are not sure where to go for the right advice. Others seem to have the strange idea that if they make a will it will somehow make them die sooner!

I have also seen families torn apart because, while the parents did some succession planning, perhaps even taking measures which were perfectly sensible and appropriate, they didn't explain to their children what that entailed. There used to be an attitude among farmers, admittedly less common now, along the lines of 'It's my business and they will get to know in good time how my estate will be divided and what each of them will inherit.' In other words, the family will get to know only after his death.

I have heard myself saying these things hundreds of times, but *nothing divides families more than money* and *it's when someone gets a nasty shock after a death that real problems occur.*

There are some children of farmers who expect to receive an

equal share of the estate (the main asset of which is of course usually the farm) and who get very upset when that doesn't happen, even going so far as to challenge their parents' wills, when the truth is that:

a. the sibling who is to get the farm has worked very hard (often since leaving school and for very little reward), having thereby contributed very significantly to its growth and increased value, or even to its continued existence as a viable business;

b. the business will not be able to continue in the future unless the farming sibling receives the bulk of the farming assets, or is at the very least given the use of them for so long as he or she carries on farming; and

c. that is what the parents most wanted to happen.

It can sometimes be the case that if the parents tell their non-farming children what they will receive, and when, the children might not always like what they are hearing, but at least they will know where they stand and will not spend the next twenty or thirty years wrongly assuming that they are going to receive an equal inheritance. They will then be able to plan their lives accordingly.

In my experience, cases like that were very much in the minority, because the non-farming children will usually not expect to receive an equal inheritance in the kinds of circumstances which I have described. Some will actually tell their parents that they don't expect to receive anything and that any inheritance which comes their way will be regarded by them as a bonus. While virtually all parents will still wish to find a way of leaving the non-farming children a fair inheritance, hearing that can come to them as a huge relief, because they have worried about it for years and have not known what to do for the best, and still less what to say to their children.

This sort of thing can of course also work the other way. My colleagues and I are still coming across situations in which a family member has been encouraged to stay working on the farm, often being paid little or nothing by way of a wage, all against the vague promise or understanding that the farm will be left to him or her in due course, only for it to emerge that the farmer never made a will, or worse still made one and left the farm to someone else. Fortunately, there can be a remedy for the disinherited child/ worker, under a principle known as 'proprietary estoppel', but success in making such a claim (which is an expensive process) will inevitably depend on the amount and quality of the evidence available, and in particular the evidence about any promise which had been made, which may often never have been put in writing.

Whatever the situation in any given case, it must surely be better for the parents to tell their children what they are planning to do and why, than for them to say nothing and leave the children in ignorance. It goes to show that effective communication is absolutely vital, so what I say to farming families is, 'For goodness' sake *talk* to each other!'

When a solicitor is acting for farmers it is necessary to understand that they will always want value for money. Thankfully, the more commercially minded farmers do tend to recognise that you get what you pay for, and that good advice doesn't come cheap but will pay for itself in due course.

There are, however, still some farmers who will try to knock you down whatever the fee quote, and they will try to agree a fixed fee quote even if that is not really appropriate for the type of matter in hand. They are usually very easy to spot, because when they ring, the first thing they do is to ask how much it will cost, sometimes even before they have explained what advice or assistance they are seeking! Experience also shows that once they have nailed you to the floor on fees they are the very people who are never off the phone, asking for constant updates, even if there hasn't been enough time for anything significant to happen. Frankly, there comes a point when, as a solicitor trying to do your best, there are some clients you are simply better off not having on the books. Fortunately, people like that are still very much the exception and I do still have plenty of happy stories to tell and even a happy ending or two to relate.

For example, one farming family who are clients of mine had a lovely surprise when the landlord of their farm died. They are truly nice people and very good farmers, but I don't think that even they expected the landlord to leave the farm to them. That restored my faith in humanity (for a while at least), and it really could not have happened to better people.

A notable thing about farming communities is that there is still a huge amount of respect when a farmer dies, particularly if he (or she) was well known. I have been to many funerals of farmers over the years, and more often than not the church has been packed and the funeral has been a major social occasion. One which stands out in my mind was that of Bill Robinson, a retired farmer from Treales, near Preston. Bill was a grand chap and, as expected, there was standing room only at the back of the parish church.

The first notable thing that day was that the Order of Service had been printed back to front, so that it opened the opposite way from normal. The vicar began the service by explaining that if anyone was thinking that a mistake had been made they were wrong, and that the Order of Service had been printed that way on purpose, because Bill had never read a book or a newspaper from the first page in his life – he had *always* started at the back page. How wonderful!

The other thing was that, not long before Bill died, his family had donated a plot of land to the church, to enable the church to extend the graveyard, which was becoming full. How fitting it was that Bill was laid to rest in the first plot in the new section of the graveyard, interred with his feet pointing directly across the road to the family farm. A lovely tribute to a lovely man.

The Royal Agricultural Benevolent Institution

For confidential help and advice call the RABI helpline on 0300 3037373 or e-mail grants@rabi.org.uk or visit the website www.rabi.org.uk
The North West regional manager, Georgina Lamb, can be contacted on 07917 114250 or by e-mail: georgina.lamb@rabi.org.uk

Farm Community Network

For more information about FCN visit www.fcn.org.uk
If you would like to contact FCN for help, or on behalf of someone who needs help, call the FCN helpline on 0845 367 9990

CHAPTER SEVEN

SOME OF MY BEST FRIENDS ARE YORKSHIREMEN

People who helped me along the way

I am a proud Lancastrian. My roots are here, and I have lived in Lancashire for the vast majority of my life. I believe that Lancashire folk are the salt of the earth – hard-working (most of them!), tough, hospitable, friendly, loyal – and funny; but I must admit, Yorkshire folk aren't far behind.

I'm as ready as the next Lancastrian to poke fun at Yorkies, and to make jokes at their expense (let's face it, there are plenty of jokes like that and lots of Yorkies to be aimed at) but (whisper it, please) I do actually like the beggars. It is true of course that some Yorkies have an inbuilt tendency to be miserable and tight-fisted, but that just gives the good folk on our side of th'ill more chances to laugh at their expense.

Seriously, over my years in the law I have met some wonderful people in Yorkshire (and Cumbria too), and that is not just Lankies over there on holiday (or 'missionary duty' as we like to call it), in case that's what you were thinking. Many of the Yorkshire farmer clients I have met have been great people and just as kind and hospitable as anyone I have met anywhere else, and even more so in some cases. They tend to be guarded and reticent at first, but I have never minded the fact that I have had to earn their respect, and hopefully then their trust. I have honestly felt completely at ease on the many occasions when I have found myself sitting in a farmhouse kitchen in the Dales, for example.

One Yorkie in particular stands out from the crowd and he leads the pack by some distance. He is my very good friend Alastair Cromarty, a specialist farm accountant who practises in Skipton, but plays golf at Harrogate. We first came across each other when we happened to be acting for some mutual farmer clients near Clitheroe, over twenty years ago, and possibly as many as twenty-five. We hit it off immediately and have been good friends ever since. I think that is probably largely because we are similar in many ways and have a shared outlook on all sorts of things. We both grew up on farms and have always loved acting for farmers. We are both sports mad and have played golf together countless times and have also been on quite a few trips together to watch golf or rugby.

Alastair has been particularly helpful to me professionally and has referred lots of farming clients to me over the years. If he was pressed, I know he would say that it's because he could be confident that I would always deal with things promptly and get them right, because he has told me so. Nevertheless, I have been very grateful for his consistent support and friendship and I only hope that I have provided a good service to the clients he has entrusted to me, and that I have been able to meet their expectations.

I really do hope that Alastair and I will stay in touch with each other after I have retired. After all, there is still a lot of golf to be played and there are plenty of golf and rugby trips waiting to be planned!

Alastair is older than me, but he has no plans to retire just yet, so if there are any farmers in Yorkshire looking for a good accountant who understands farmers, you now know where to go.

Of course there have been plenty of other Yorkshire folk who have helped me and whose friendship I have enjoyed. For example, three who spring to mind are the lads at Skipton Auction: Chris Windle, Michael Beech and Adam Winthrop; three men who have always done a professional job with a smile on their faces. There are others, but rather than start making a long list I will just say here that I have appreciated your support and that you will know who you are.

Many other people have helped me one way or another during my career. There have also been others who did not help me when they could have done so and probably should have, but why waste time and effort mentioning them?

I know lists are dangerous, because there is always the risk of missing out someone who should have been mentioned, and thereby causing offence, but these are my memoirs after all, so I'm going to risk it and now mention the names of some of the other people who have played a significant role in my professional life, some of whom have already been mentioned in this book, and at least one of whom is deceased:

Eric Sagar

My primary school headmaster, who took the trouble to give me private tuition rather than allowing me to go to grammar school a year early.

Bernie Coates

My history teacher and mentor at grammar school, who gave me an interest in history, and who steered me towards Durham University and the study of law.

John Woosnam

John has been one of my partners in Napthens ever since the firm merged with Houghton Craven & Dickson in 1990. He was a great source of help and encouragement to me, particularly in the early days when we were working together at Garstang and especially when I wasn't sure about something or had got something wrong. Thanks for your wise counsel, mate.

Various referrers of business

There have been plenty of these and I am grateful to every one of them for entrusting their clients or members to my care. I just hope that most of you still think it was worth it! There have been accountants and land agents, bank managers, farm consultants, planning consultants, NFU people, and many more.

Among the NFU people, Steve Heaton, Andrew Rothwell and Robert Sheasby stand out. Steve for first suggesting in 1989 that Napthens might have a link to the NFU; Andrew for being a consistent referrer of legal issues to my colleagues and myself over many years; and Robert for being particularly positive towards my firm since he became Regional Director.

Some of the bank managers who have been especially helpful are people like Nick Marsh, Malcolm Robinson, David Maughan, Mark Pearson and Gordon Whitford, but there have been many more. As well as Alastair Cromarty, the roll of honour in the accounting world would have to include the likes of Michael Lucas, William Richmond, David Kirkhope, Jonathan Cross, Diane Eatough, Grahame Sewell, Rob Hitch and James Cornthwaite.

Apart from the guys at Skipton I have mentioned already, land agents who have come up with the goods, and in many cases have offered friendship, are people like Richard Furnival, David

Cowburn and James Fish, Adam Pickervance, Paul Johnson, Alan Bowe, Paul Wilson, Andrew Coney, Andrew Thompson and Simon Mair, Richard Turner and Paul Dennis, and John Hughes and Michael Mashiter.

Thank you all. I have tried to reciprocate whenever that has been possible, but I hope that I have always been fair and even-handed and that I have done a good job for your clients.

Finally, it would be wrong of me not to mention some of the secretarial staff who have worked for me, but who have not already been mentioned in this book. I have spoken of the dedicated support staff who worked with me at Garstang, but of course there have been many others who have helped me at other offices during my career.

One such was Sandra Barrow, a wonderful lady whose strong Christian faith was evident in everything she said or did and who was a good friend during the six or so years when she worked for me in Preston; another was Ravinderjit Johal (who liked to be known as Sharon), a charming young woman who was always friendly and conscientious and who worked in the team at Preston for a year or two before she and her family returned to their roots in the West Midlands; then there was Lorraine Lister, who transferred to the rural team from another department within the firm to replace Sandra and worked for me part-time for about 18 months, including virtually the whole of the time I spent working out of our Blackburn office. She was such a cheerful and willing soul that it was a pleasure to have her on the team. It would also be wrong not to mention Jean Nuttall, another more mature lady who was a part-time member of the team at Preston; and then more recently we were joined by Fiona Roberts and Catherine Riley at Blackburn, and Catherine Peake at Penrith, all of whom quickly proved to be *good 'uns* as well;

last but not least was Tania Williams, who has been with the firm for a long time and worked in the rural team for many years, but is now a receptionist at the firm's head office in Preston. A tireless worker and organiser and in many ways a leader among her peers, Tania was always a great example to others in the way she went about her work, but she still found time to be the life and soul of the party.

Thank you all for putting up with me!

CHAPTER EIGHT

IF A MAN TELLS YOU HIS WORD IS AS GOOD AS HIS BOND

Collected wisdom

I have always enjoyed collecting pithy sayings or quotations. I 'borrow' them habitually too because, as the saying goes, *'Borrowing from one person is plagiarism, but borrowing from many people is research'*! In this chapter I consider a few of my favourites and some of the contexts in which I have found them helpful, or at least relevant.

> *'If a man tells you his word is as good as his bond – take his bond.'*
>
> Groucho Marx

This makes the point with humour, doesn't it, and in just a few words? Some farmers still find this principle hard to understand because, in many areas of farming life and commerce, deals are still done on a handshake or a nod, or in accordance with local custom. In a sense, that's really how things should be, and part of me wishes

135

that it could safely be like that all the time. However, years of experience as a solicitor have convinced me that it is in truth always better for farmers to get their deals and their affairs documented properly. I have seen too many things go wrong disastrously, simply because someone didn't bother to have a proper will, or a simple agreement recording the terms of the family partnership, for example. Sometimes the failure to address important issues has been because of misplaced concern over the perceived cost of doing things properly, or lack of proper guidance, or even just sheer ignorance of the risks involved. The outcome can be years of stress, a family torn apart, and huge legal bills. I have witnessed that too many times and my litigation colleagues have all too often had the very difficult task of trying to resolve a mess that could have been avoided.

Of course, there will always be some farmers who will fail to take the appropriate action even after they have received the right advice, and even after the potential consequences of inaction have been spelled out to them in the starkest of terms. That can be very sad, but in the last analysis the situation then ceased to be my problem. My job has been to offer the right advice, and if the client failed to take it, that was his problem and not mine, so I could then move on from that matter with a clear conscience.

'I know it can't be equal, but I want it to be fair.'

Anon

This was said to me by a very shrewd farmer client a few years ago. I had been discussing with him and his wife what provision they should make in their wills for their two sons. One was married with children, but lived away from the farm and had nothing to do with the business. The other was in his mid-thirties and unmarried, fully involved in the family dairy-farming business

and very unlikely ever to do anything else. I had explained all the options which the parents might wish to consider, but they had clearly understood that, given their particular circumstances, for the farming son to be able to continue the business in the long term he would ultimately have to have (or at least have the use of) the bulk of their assets in terms of value, and that they would have to find other ways of making fair provision for their other son.

That has to be the norm in many farming situations and it is usually understood and accepted by the whole family, including the non-farming children, but often completely misunderstood by people not connected with farming, including (I'm afraid to say) many lawyers, some of whom even claim to be experts. The major proviso is that I always stress that if at all possible the parents absolutely must discuss their plans openly with all their family.

'Nothing divides families more than money.'

'It's when someone gets a nasty shock [about the terms of a will] after a death that real problems occur.'
Geoff Tomlinson

These are two phrases I have uttered very many times when I have been explaining to farming parents the importance of disclosing to all of their children what each of them will inherit in due course and (if it is the case) why that might not be equal in terms of value.

As I have explained, in many cases the non-farming children will volunteer that they have always understood that their sibling would be bequeathed the farm, sometimes adding that they have made their own way in life (often having already received financial help from mum and dad when they needed it most, perhaps when they were buying a house or starting a business), and that any inheritance they may receive in due course will be regarded by them as a bonus, so their parents must stop worrying about it. That isn't always the case, but when it is, it lifts a huge burden from the shoulders of the parents, who may have been worrying about the issue for years.

There are occasions when the non-farming children are unhappy when they are told that their parents have planned to leave them less than their sibling, but at least they will know where they stand and will not spend the next few decades wrongly assuming that they will receive an equal inheritance.

Like many important things in life, this issue is really all about effective communication, and most farming folk do see the point. On a practical level, if all the family know where they stand, that should reduce the risk in due course of a challenge being made to the will, which can be very unpleasant for the whole family, and of course extremely expensive.

'There is no limit to what can be achieved if you don't mind who gets the credit.'
Ronald Reagan, 40th President of the
United States of America

Ronald Reagan had something of an image of being a bumbling idiot, particularly in the later years of his life, but in reality he was a very intelligent and articulate man, and some of the things he said or wrote are well worth reading. The above quotation was apparently on a plaque on his desk in the Oval Office when he was President, although I believe it was originally said by Harry S. Truman, 33rd President; and a similar quote is also attributed to Bob Woodruff, CEO of Coca-Cola, 1926–1954.

For me, this little maxim sums up the essence of teamwork, and I believe the world would be a better place if more people lived by it. The converse is also true: that no team can work to its optimum if one member seeks to hog the credit all of the time, particularly if he or she is supposed to be the leader.

> *'Management is efficiency in climbing the ladder of success; leadership determines whether the ladder is leaning against the right wall.'*
>
> STEVEN COVEY, AMERICAN BUSINESSMAN (BORN 1932)

Good leadership is essential in all walks of life, whether in business, politics or sport, or indeed in church life, but many people don't understand the difference between leadership and management, and I think this saying explains it very succinctly. Managers are important, but their job is to implement the strategy which has been set by the leaders, to work out how to do something and not whether or not it should be done in the first place. By definition, there will be far fewer leaders than managers, and problems occur when, for whatever reason, the boundaries become blurred. If you think you are a leader, the acid test is to look behind you every now and then to see if anyone is following. That will tell you all you need to know.

Some people try to lead by force of personality. That was the style of Peter Hosker, senior partner in my firm when I was a young partner in the 1980s. His favourite phrase when an important decision had to be made in a partners' meeting was, 'I'm quite prepared to be in the minority, but I think we should...' All the other partners understood that what he actually meant was, 'Do it my way, or suffer the consequences!' To his credit, Peter was usually right and he did achieve a lot for the firm in those days, dragging the rest of us along with him through what I suppose were the early stages of modernisation. His style worked for a season, but ultimately it did lead to resentment.

I understand that sometimes a leader needs to stand firm and that he or she will usually need to set the tone and will often then have to convince others of the wisdom of buying in to what is proposed, but in the last analysis I believe that working by genuine consensus will always be better for all concerned, and more effective in the long run.

'Machinery doesn't create energy; it consumes it.'

ANON

I'm afraid I don't know who first said this, but I would like to know. Having the appropriate structure within any business is of course very important. It should be one which gives the workers at the coalface, the wealth creators, all the tools they need to do the job with maximum effectiveness, but I do think that I cannot be the only one who believes that we have managed in our society to allow things to get out of balance over the last twenty years or so. We spend too much time and energy (and money) on secondary issues. Of course we do need management alongside HR, Accounts, IT, Marketing and so on, but we should never forget that they are a means to an end, not an end in themselves. Understandably, people who work in those areas may well feel the opposite is true for them, as that is how they earn their livelihood, but the bigger picture tells us otherwise.

I know it may sound cynical of me to say this, but it can be useful to remember that IT and Marketing people do have a vested interest in changing everything as often as they can possible justify it and sometimes even when they can't. They call it 're-branding' or 'upgrading'. It's nothing personal, folks, and perhaps it's just the view of an ageing and soon-to-be-retired solicitor who grew tired of having to learn new things all the time, but I do think I have a point. Anything that helped me and my colleagues provide a better service to our clients was of course very welcome, but that had to be the benchmark; and anything which consumed a disproportionate amount of time had to be questioned and would be unwelcome if the end result did not help improve performance and in particular the speed and quality of service provided to the most important people in the organisation, its clients.

'Allus stand back of a shooter, front of a sh*ter.'
OLD LANCASHIRE SAYING

Sound advice, direct and to the point, in typical Lancashire style.

'You spell rugby F-U-N, but it's an awful lot (sic) more fun when you're winning.'
J.R.H. Greenwood, former England rugby captain and coach

Richard (Dick) Greenwood (father of England World Cup winning centre and now Sky Sports rugby pundit Will) said this to me when he was coaching my team, Preston Grasshoppers, just a year or two before he became England coach. It was typical of the witty and perceptive quips which were his trademark, and it was great fun to train and play under him (although in truth I didn't play many games in the first team, even in that period) and I learned a lot.

Dick's comment summed up very accurately the attitude of most people in the world of amateur sport which I inhabited. One of the best aspects of rugby union has always been that after the game we were all mates and would always have a drink with our opposition, but on the pitch we would always try our very hardest to win and would enjoy it more when we did. How true, Dick; how true.

Chapter Nine

TOP TIPS FOR ASPIRING AGRICULTURAL LAWYERS

Lessons learned and principles
I have established

This is a re-worked and expanded version of a series which first appeared in my firm's rural newsletter. It contains advice which I had gleaned from my long career as a specialist agricultural solicitor and which is essentially practical in nature. It is intended to help and encourage in particular those who are hoping to embark on a similar career, but if it is useful to those who have already set off on that journey, so much the better.

1. Go to the farm whenever possible

I have been amazed over the years by how many solicitors have tried to deal with farming matters without actually visiting the site. Visits to farms take time, which will have to be written off if you don't get the job, and you may not be able to charge for it even if you are instructed, but it will still be worth the effort. You won't necessarily have to go to the farm every time you need to see the client, but do always offer to go for the first meeting. It will give the farmer a very strong message that you are interested in him and that you are prepared to put yourself out. If it will help, offer to go early in the morning or in the evening, which may be more convenient for the farmer.

A site visit may be essential in some cases, for example if the issue is a boundary or access dispute, but I would also usually want to visit if I was to be instructed to act on the sale of all or part of the farm, particularly if land was to be sold in lots. It's far easier to understand what is intended if you have seen the property on the ground than if you are trying to deal with it purely on the basis of paper plans, especially if you have had a joint visit with the client and his (or her) land agent. I have sometimes been able to give valuable input into the lotting proposals, for example, because of issues such as the location of the best access (which the deeds might even show is shared with another property), or the position of the nearest available water main.

Even in cases where no such issue arises, a visit to the farm can immediately tell me a lot about the farm and about the people running it. Is it busy, or quiet – even devoid of animals or machinery? Does it give the impression of being workmanlike and efficient, with everything in its place, yet clearly in full use, or is it untidy and uncared for, with old and broken-down machinery all over the place? What type of farm is it anyway? Are the farm buildings old-fashioned or are they up to date and perhaps only very recently constructed? Are there older buildings with obvious potential for conversion and, if so, do they still appear to be in use and for what?

1a. Check the map before you go
At the very least check and even print out an online map such as Google Maps, because knowing your route before you set off

to visit a farm will reduce any risk of you being late. Remember that satnav isn't always correct in country areas; but Google Earth can be a very helpful means of working out the location of the farmhouse within the site (which isn't always obvious), and the best means of access to it. Bear in mind too that not all farms have a sign at the end of their road or at the entrance to the farmyard.

I once had difficulty finding the farmhouse on my first visit to a farm in a moorland setting. I drove down the road and into the yard, but I couldn't see the house, only a large brick barn in front of me. I looked to my left and concluded at once that the route to the house couldn't be that way, because it was a yard full of cows. To my right, at the end of the brick barn in front of me, was a Dutch barn, but there was still no sign of the house. And then I looked up and saw some chimneys over the top of the brick barn. That meant that the house must be on the other side of the barn, but how did I get to it? In front of me was an open doorway, so I went through it. There was a passageway to my right, at the end of which, through another open door, I could see a milking parlour, so the house clearly wasn't down there. There was another door in front of me, so I decided that the house must be at the other side of it. I opened it and went through, to be greeted by the entire family gathered around the fire in what was clearly their sitting room! 'Come in, lad, and have a cup of tea!' was the cheery greeting from the dad.

1b. Be punctual

Allow plenty of time for potential traffic problems. You can always park up near the farm to make some calls if you get there too early, but remember, it's always better to be ten minutes early than five minutes late. Being late gives the farmer a very bad message from the start.

1c. Be prepared to be flexible when fixing times

This is because it is best to fit in with the daily (or seasonal) schedule on the farm, which will vary depending on the type of farming carried on there. For example, there is no point expecting to be seen at milking time on a dairy farm (although that is beginning to be less of an issue now as more dairy farms are switching to robotic milking systems). Also, don't be surprised if the farmer re-schedules the meeting, for example if the weather has improved after a long spell of bad weather which has prevented him from making a start on harvest, or silage-making; and understand that it may take several attempts to get some farmers to fix a meeting at all.

1d. Choose carefully where you park in the farmyard

It might not be very clean!

1e. Take your wellies

Always have your wellies in the boot of your car, or better still in the front, just in case you forget the preceding rule. I have fallen foul (literally) of that one once or twice.

1f. Accept hospitality

On arrival you will usually be offered a cup of tea or coffee, often accompanied by a selection of home-baking (or even more, as I described in chapter six). As a general rule, it's not a good idea to risk causing offence by refusing – but there are exceptions, of course! I have been in some very untidy and, frankly, dirty farmhouse kitchens over the years, even one or two with hens wandering around inside! When offered a cup of tea in a place like that the diplomatic response is, 'No thanks, I've just had one.'

2. Be prepared

Preparation is vital. If there is a file, read it. If not, check what you already know about the farm, the farmer and his family, and thereby at least make sure that you have an idea of the issue or issues likely to be under discussion. You should be able to get some helpful basic information from your note of your initial telephone conversation with the potential client when the meeting was arranged (it is important to get that information at that stage if at all possible) or from whatever briefing note you have been given if the meeting was set up for you by a colleague. If the initial information you have is inadequate, ring the client to ask for it. He is very unlikely to mind you doing that.

Arriving for the meeting having done at least some preparation should save time (which the farmer will appreciate) and once again it sends the strong message that you are interested in that particular person. I have had colleagues (in other departments within my firm) who, when asked to identify their most important client, would say the one who brings in the most fees every year. I disagreed fundamentally with that view. For me, my most important client has always been the one with whom I was dealing at any given moment. It's a matter of your viewpoint, I suppose, but in my view that is the very essence of good client service.

3. Listen

Listening has not always been my greatest strength, as my wife constantly reminds me. The principle is not to try to give advice before you know and understand the question. Therein lies the risk of making a completely wrong assumption about what the client really wants or needs. If you try to dictate the discussion, that can quickly lead to disaster, and many farmers will dismiss very quickly what they see as the 'city attitude' of some solicitors. Instead, ask pertinent questions and wait for the answers before moving on; the single most important question being to ask the farmer to identify what he wants to achieve as a result of the exercise on which he may be about to embark. He may not yet have worked that out for himself, but it is of course fundamental to know where you want to go before you start trying to work out how to get there, and asking that question can often lead to a fruitful discussion. Of course, the answer may be so obvious in some cases that it does not even need to be spelled out, for example if the matter is the straightforward purchase of a piece of land. In other cases, it could be that no further progress can be made until the end in view is identified and agreed, for example in a complicated farm succession case, so at the end of the first meeting the client may have to be left to think about that before confirming his instructions.

Getting to the heart of an issue as soon as is reasonably possible (after the usual initial pleasantries) will benefit everyone, as it will save your time and therefore the client's money.

4. Don't be pushy

Advise the client of any deadline he must meet, but otherwise give him time to mull things over if necessary.

5. Be honest

Admit it if you don't know the answer to a question, but offer to find out or to ask a colleague, or explain that you will need time to think about it, but that you will confirm your advice very soon, within the next few days if at all possible.

Remember, farmers know bull***t when they see it.

6. Address the issue of cost

The client will want to know the likely cost of your services. In the unlikely event of him not asking, it is a good idea to volunteer the information. Give your best estimate and/or set an initial budget with a promise to review it once that is reached, or is approaching rapidly; or say that you will confirm your estimate in writing within a specified timescale, and explain that a formal terms-of-business/client care letter will follow in any event. If possible, ensure that the client understands that, just as he will want to know how much it will cost, you will want to know how you will be paid and when.

7. Keep your promises

Turn up on time. Write when you say you will. Return phone calls as soon as you can. Simple stuff, I know, but vital if you want to be considered trustworthy and reliable. Sadly, far too many of us have had the unfortunate experience of dealing with other professionals or with financial institutions that don't follow these basic rules. Banks and insurance companies are the worst culprits at the moment and sadly some of them provide a level of service which is completely unacceptable.

There are also some solicitors who are unreliable and even rude, who are hardly ever available when you need them, who rarely return calls promptly and who are generally unhelpful. These are people who are supposedly trying to make a living out of the law! It's hard to comprehend but, believe me, they are still out there. If you are a solicitor, you wouldn't want to be grouped with them, would you?

8. Follow up the first meeting promptly

As soon as possible after your first meeting with a new client, confirm in writing the matters discussed, the issues raised and any initial advice given. Do this at length if necessary. It's best to cover everything at the start because a) you might otherwise forget some salient points and b) the letter will serve as a useful aide-memoire for you (and for the client) when you come back to the file, which could be weeks or even months later if the client is slow to confirm your instructions. With the client's permission, do also send a copy of the letter to anyone else who was at the meeting, such as the accountant or another family member, if this is appropriate.

9. Don't forget your thank-yous

If you were introduced to the new client by a third party, such as an accountant, land agent or bank manager, don't forget to write and say thank you for the introduction. It is only common courtesy to do so, but if you forget the third party may not bother to mention your name the next time he or she gets a similar opportunity.

10. Final points

10a. Know your stuff
This should go without saying, but do keep up to date with changes in the law.

10b. Keep up with trends and changes in farming
Read the farming press and attend appropriate seminars and meetings, and you may then be able to anticipate particular developments which may affect your farming clients. In short, be aware of the issues which are foremost in the minds of farmers at any given time.

10c. Don't claim to be an expert
That is for others to decide. As far as you are concerned, 'specialist' will do. Remember the saying, *'An ex is a has-been and a spurt is a drip under pressure!'*

10d. Above all, BE YOURSELF
Most farmers simply don't appreciate airs and graces.

CHAPTER TEN

A MOST EFFECTIVE BOWLER

My lifelong obsession with sport

S ome readers of these memoirs (or at least those who have known me for some time) may find it difficult to imagine that anyone would describe me as 'a most effective bowler', because they will never have thought of me as a cricketer. Admittedly, I was only thirteen at the time and those words were said as a result of a small measure of success I had enjoyed in what was only a junior inter-house match at my grammar school, but what was said did encourage me, even if no one else was particularly impressed. Junior competitions were for boys in the first three years at Kirkham Grammar School (the third form, lower fourth form and upper fourth form, in the archaic language used by the school back then). I was in the second year and had opened the bowling with a third-year boy, David Rawcliffe, who really was a handy bowler. The opposition must not have been very good, because we bowled them out for the grand total of 14 and David took 6–3 while I took 3–6. The comment about my prowess was made by our housemaster, Bill McKerrow, in my end-of-term

report. He was a nice chap; a physics teacher (of sorts) and ex-RAF, complete with his splendid handlebar moustache.

I did enjoy cricket and I was a reasonable bowler at school, but in truth that performance in the summer of 1967 was probably the highlight of my cricketing career and as far as I ever got in the game. I bowled medium pace at best, with a bit of swing and a bit of seam and even the occasional bit of off-spin. I was self-taught – I had to be, because no one at school ever gave us any coaching. I was never even taught how I was supposed to hold the ball and so I had to work it out for myself. In the summer term cricket was very popular and my friends and I would have lots of impromptu games during our lunch breaks. However, apart from the odd house match, cricket never went much further than that for me when I was at school. I was a good enough runner to be part of the school athletics team, so there wasn't time to play cricket as well. I never played club cricket either, but I did enjoy playing social cricket for the office team many years later, in the 1990s. For a number of years we would play about half a dozen 20-over matches on summer evenings, against firms of accountants and land agents and so on. I enjoyed bowling in them, but I never could bat and my highest ever score was probably no more than about 10.

A couple of abiding memories from my days playing social cricket come from the annual six-a-side tournament which was held at the Oyster Festival at Guy's Thatched Hamlet at Bilsborrow near Preston in early September. We entered a team every year in the early days and I think I played just about every time. There were usually about six to eight teams and the way it worked was that each team provided five players of its own but was joined by an ex-professional, or sometimes a young overseas professional who was playing in the local leagues. They came from a pool of four such players who were recruited by the organisers every year, and they included some notable old players, people like former Lancashire stars Jack Simmons, Ken Snellgrove and Peter 'Leapy' Lee, who was the leading wicket-taker in English county cricket in 1973. The tournaments were great fun and no one took them too seriously, although sometimes the pros would step things up a notch if one of the amateurs was beginning to take liberties.

We usually had one or two good players (sometimes 'borrowed' for the purpose), but most of us were just occasional cricketers. Despite that, we did win occasionally. Our best player by far was Pat Newell, a top-class wicket-keeper batsman who had been on Lancashire's books as a junior and played for Blackpool in the Northern League for about fifteen years. For me, it was a privilege to play with and against men who had played at a very high level in their time, but the real highlights were when I had Jack Simmons caught behind (he didn't think he'd hit it, but the umpire did and that's all that counted – look in the scorebook, Jack!) and clean-bowled Ken Snellgrove (middle stump) with a ball that was a yard quicker than the previous one and nipped back off the seam (yes, I can see it now!). However, Ken got his revenge in the final of the tournament one year. I was batting and we needed two runs to win off the last ball, and Ken was bowling. I took a stride down the pitch and hit the ball as hard as I could, but unfortunately it went straight back at Ken; although he didn't catch it he knocked it down and ran me out. A yard either side of Ken and it would have gone for four – but as I said, I never could bat.

I have always enjoyed watching cricket and over the years I have been to watch the odd one-day international, or a day of a Test Match at Old Trafford, Headingley or Trent Bridge, but not for some years now, although I do still watch some cricket on television. The last international match I attended was a one-day match between England and Pakistan at Headingley with my son Andy when he was in his final year at Leeds University. At the time he was sharing a house only a few hundred yards from the ground, so it was really convenient. He now lives in Brixton, which isn't very far from The Oval, and we have both said that we should go to an international match there some time, but haven't yet managed it. I would obviously also love to attend a match at Lord's – another thing on my 'Bucket List' – but so far I have only visited the ground. That was one winter when Paul Johnson, a land agent I have known and worked with for many years, very kindly took me as his guest. Paul is a member of MCC and also of the MCC Golf Society, and we attended the tenth anniversary dinner of that society, held in the Long Room at Lord's, no less! We got there early and had time to look around the Cricket Museum and the members' areas of the Pavilion. The whole thing was an amazing experience for me. Thanks, Paul!

In cricket terms I think the ultimate treat for me would be to go to watch at least part of an England tour to the West Indies, such as the Test in Barbados. One day perhaps!

As I have mentioned, when I was at school I was quite a good runner. In winter we did cross-country and, like my dad, who had been a good cross-country runner at KGS, I had the right build for it. In the summer term we did athletics and cricket, but it wasn't physically possible to be in both teams, so it was athletics for me. For some reason I was quite good at the long jump, so I did that in the inter-house competition on Sports Day (and the triple jump and the sprint relays), but my main event was the 800 metres, the metric equivalent of the old half-mile. My dad had been a very good half-miler and achieved a narrow victory on Sports Day in 1942, thus setting a new school record for the half-mile which, converted to a metric time, still stood in 1972, when I was the fastest 800-metre runner in my year. The rule was that school records could be set only on Sports Day itself, but there was every reason to believe that I could achieve the feat, especially as I had actually bettered the (converted) time in a match against another school only the week before. When Sports Day came, dad was there watching, as indeed was Sid Crane, a teacher who had taught dad and had seen him set his record and who was still teaching at KGS. Not much pressure on me then!

Sadly, I wasn't up to it. I didn't pace myself and I went off far too quickly, anxious as I was to set a new record time. I blew up before the end and I didn't even win the race. Needless to say, that was the end of my track-and-field career and I never ran another 800-metre race. That was probably no bad thing, because I had already realised that I wasn't in fact all that quick. My best ever time was only about 2 minutes 7.5 seconds, and I had experienced competing in inter-school races against other boys who were running the 800 metres in under 2 minutes. Furthermore, there was an athlete in the year above me, Pete Beavan, who would have become a top-level runner if injury hadn't intervened, and he would probably have run in the 1972 Olympics. At the age of 17 he had won the European under-20 400-metres final in 47 seconds, so if he had wanted he could have smashed the school 800-metres record a couple of years before my feeble attempt.

As you will have gathered, I have always loved sport and it has played a significant part in my life and hopefully that will continue for a few more years yet. Golf is now my main sporting activity, although since my teens I have also enjoyed walking the Lake District fells. I haven't been on the fells very often in recent years but hope to get back to walking them, that is, if my fragile back will allow me.

When I was about nine or ten I loved football, and my ambition was to become a professional footballer. I don't suppose for a moment that I would have been good enough even if the chance had come my way, but I was quite a handy goal-scorer as a kid (or so I thought anyway), and in my early teens I was quite tall for my age and fairly quick, so I usually managed to play centre-forward.

I used to spend hours on my own in the yard at the farm practising my dribbling, passing, heading and shooting (especially the shooting). I was also determined that I would be 'two-footed' like my great hero Tom Finney, so I concentrated on shooting, passing and crossing with my weaker foot, the left one. In time, that became second nature and it also came in handy many years later when I was playing fly-half at rugby, because it was very useful to be able to kick to touch with my left foot when I was under pressure in defence. I also even managed to kick a couple of left-footed drop goals in my time. When aged fifteen, I started playing for the adult village football team, and I felt quite comfortable playing on the left wing, which is where I was often put when I did actually get a game. That was in my home village of Woodplumpton (I believe the name derives from the fact that it was originally an Anglo-Saxon settlement) in the Catforth & District Summer Football League; a league which was started in the 1920s to give farm boys a chance to play competitive games in leagues. In those days they were all working on Saturdays, and in winter it was too dark to play after work during the week, but of course that problem didn't exist in the summer months.

When I first started to play, only players who lived in the defined league area (which was all rural) were allowed to play, although they could play for any team in the league. However, that rule began to be relaxed and soon young men from the towns, probably all of whom were already playing all through the winter season anyway, started appearing in the teams. That changed the dynamic dramatically and it was never quite the same after that. Until then it was still essentially country lads and it really didn't matter that the standard wasn't very high.

In any event, I played on and off for a few years, including during my summers at home from university, and then I had a year or two playing for Catforth second team in the second division of the league. The football was fairly agricultural, to say the least, and the facilities ranged from minimal to non-existent. It was quite normal to change into our playing kit in our cars, and there were usually no showers or anything fancy like that, and certainly no medical facilities, but none of those things bothered us at all. Having said that, we did sometimes have to move sheep or cows away from the pitch before we could play, although we obviously couldn't clear what they had left behind, which is when we would really have liked showers, or at least a cold tap!

Readers from the Pilling area will no doubt remember, or at least have heard of, the legendary Fred Jenkinson. He was from a large farming clan in the Eagland Hill area and he was a stalwart of the summer league for a very long time, first as a player and later as a referee. I remember once turning up to an away match at Eagland Hill after Fred had officially retired from playing. When we arrived we discovered that the home team were a player short, so Fred volunteered to turn out for them and he then played the whole match in jeans and proper Lancashire clogs. He didn't take prisoners at the best of times and I don't think he lost many challenges that evening!

For much of the period when I played in the summer league my good mate Jim Martin played as an attacking midfielder in the same team, and in truth he was a much better footballer than I could ever have hoped to become. I had first got to know him when I was about nine years old, because he would come to play with a primary school friend of his, Ray Stansfield, who lived in a bungalow next door to Horace Coupe's pig farm – Ray being the same friend I mentioned back in chapter six and Horace being the owner of the Alsatian that bit my bum! Jim and Ray were both Catholics, so they attended a different school from mine, but our two schools shared a bus for regular trips to Kirkham Swimming Baths (which I hated) and that's how I first got to know them. They were both a year older than me, but we would spend many happy hours playing football together in the field next to Ray's parents' bungalow. I don't know what happened to Ray, but Jim and I are still mates some fifty years later.

We also played football in the playground (yard actually) at my own primary school, but we never had matches against other schools or anything like that. However, some of the older boys in the village did put a team together to play ad hoc matches against lads from other neighbouring villages, such as Catforth and Barton (where I later lived for more than seventeen years). I probably started playing for that team when I was eleven or twelve, when the oldest boys would be fifteen or sixteen, so it was quite a mix of ages, as well as of ability. We would go on our bikes to play away games in the other villages, but again there was no league and we probably only ever played a handful of matches. Jim was also in that team and Ray was our goalie.

I remember playing away to Barton in one of my first games and that we won 16–1. Because I was one of the youngest playing that day I was put at left-back, but I still managed to creep forward enough times to score a hat trick. One of the Barton team that day was a farmer's son like me, but unlike me he followed his dad into farming and many years later he became a client of mine. As you can imagine, I seized the opportunity to remind him of that match, which he had to admit he had never forgotten.

Two things prevented my career as a footballer from going any further (apart from a lack of any real talent, that is). First, when

I was twelve I had to start wearing glasses because I was really quite short-sighted. Contact lenses were around by then (it was 1966) but I guess they were still quite primitive and expensive, which was probably more to the point. I did actually manage to get by wearing glasses to play for a few years, but it made it quite difficult if I was trying to power a header into the top corner! It also wasn't easy playing rugby at grammar school without contact lenses, especially because it was difficult for me to judge distances, for example when a ball was coming through the air towards me. I finally got contact lenses when I was seventeen and that gave my sporting life a huge boost. By then football had already taken a back seat, because I had found my real love in rugby and was fully committed to that great game as my main sport for the best part of the next twenty-five years – but first, a couple more football stories.

I continued to play village football in the summer league for a few years and while I was still at school a number of my contemporaries also played football, even though it was a rugby-playing school. We organised our own team and when we were about fifteen or sixteen we once played the boys from the year above after school on one of the rugby pitches ('the Cabbage Patch' for those who remember it). We beat them, and I scored the winning goal. I also remember playing for the prefects' team against the masters' team and beating them too, and that I scored in that game as well. I still have the photos to prove that one. On a couple of occasions, when I was about fourteen, I also arranged matches against my old village team, Woodplumpton Juniors. I played for the school, but I can't remember the results.

For a good number of years, during my thirties and beyond, I did also play in outdoor five-a-side matches at West View Leisure Centre in Preston on Wednesday nights with a group of men who were loosely associated with my church. It was an area about three times the size of a five-a-side pitch and the number of players on each side depended on how many turned up on the night. Also in my thirties (I think) I played a few games of football for an office team and a couple for a church team, all of them at Preston North End's ground at Deepdale when it had a plastic pitch. The pitch was terrible, but it was still great to be able to hire it for the odd challenge match and to play in a Football League Stadium, which I probably did three or four times in all. Inevitably, my memories are of a couple of goals I scored, both at the Town End of the ground. One was the winner in a 4–3 victory, a prod over the line from a couple of yards out, but the other was a soaring jack-knife header powered into the near-post top corner from the corner of the six-yard box. I still maintain that it was probably the best headed goal ever scored at the Town End – it's just a pity that there were no spectators in the ground to see it!

With church football team, about to play on Preston North End's then plastic pitch.

When I knew that I would be going to a rugby-playing grammar school, I was quite dismayed at first. However, when I got there and it came to rugby, I tried my best and soon realised that I must have had some kind of ability, because I found myself selected for the under-12s team, initially at centre, but later at fly-half. I loved it and threw myself into the game with my usual enthusiasm, but we weren't very good and we didn't actually win a match until we were under-15s, by which time I was captain. I had also enjoyed a measure of personal success by then. At the age of thirteen I had played in the centre in a Senior House match, which meant that I was playing against much older and bigger boys, some of whom were eighteen. Nowadays, it wouldn't be allowed, but I managed all right and I did score a try. I was also receiving encouraging comments from the staff in my school reports, with phrases such as *'a very promising all-round sports player'*, *'plays well and is learning the finer points rapidly'* and *'very good, keen and capable player'*.

If I had believed those reports at the time (which I probably did, to be honest) I would have thought that I was going to become a star player in more than one sport. I eventually played in the mid-Lancashire under-15s trials (held at Preston Grasshoppers' old ground in Lea – my first ever visit to the club which later became my rugby home for most of my playing career), but I didn't get through to the next stage of the trials for the Lancashire team, so I should have suspected then that I wasn't actually quite as good a player as I had imagined. If not then, it should have begun to dawn on me a few years later, when I was the only one of six players from my school who played in the initial trials at Fylde *not* to get through to the final county trials, but I can only remember feeling that I had been hard done by. Oh, the innocence of youth!

It was slightly strange that my year team at school didn't begin to win matches until we were in our fourth year, because by the time we were in the Upper Sixth (aged seventeen and eighteen) we were winning most of our matches. Admittedly, we were helped by some outstanding players from other years, and two in particular from the year below us: Keith Aitchison ('Aitch') and Clive Hughes, both of whom went on to play for England Schools in their final year at Kirkham. Keith was picked at fly-half in the school first team when he was in the fifth year, so when I did get into the team on a regular basis I had to play at full-back, and I played there throughout my last year. Clive was a number 8 and an immensely talented all-round sportsman who was also an exceptional javelin thrower. It was devastating to hear when I was at university that Clive had been knocked down and killed in a road accident. What a huge waste of life and of a very special talent.

Another star of our school team in my last year was the captain, John Martindale. He was from the year above, but had stayed on to re-sit his A-levels (which is ironic because, perhaps through sheer persistence, he did end up with a doctorate in plant genetics). He was a very strong and quick winger and scored a lot of tries for the team. His dad, Jack, also a farmer's son who later did some farming himself, had been at KGS with my dad and in fact they were lifelong friends. I was greatly honoured when Jack asked me to give the tribute to his wife Margaret at her funeral in 2003, very shortly after my own mum's funeral, and also very pleased that Jack made the considerable effort required to be at my dad's funeral in March 2012, despite the fact that he was already elderly and not at all in good health himself. He has himself also now passed away, and I was pleased to be able to attend his funeral, along with a good number of my old rugby mates. I should perhaps mention that I hadn't always agreed with Jack, especially when he was Chairman of Selectors at Preston Grasshoppers when I was trying to hold down a place in the first team!

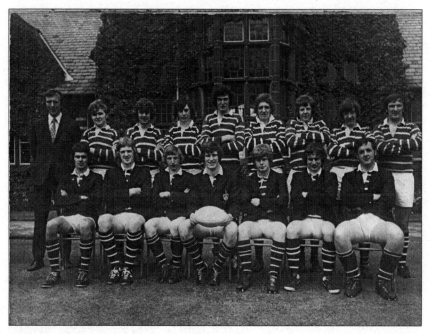

Kirkham Grammar School 1st XV, 1971-72. To my left are Clive Hughes, Keith Aitchison, John Martindale and Glen Leeming.

We also had a top-class scrum-half in our school team, Steve Berry ('Bez'), and I had the pleasure of playing fly-half outside him quite a lot at the 'Hoppers in the following years. Steve, who was also from the year below me, was another outstanding all-round sportsman and a very good cricketer (a fast bowler) in particular who played as a professional in league cricket for a few years. Bez and Aitch were a class act when they played at half-back together, and in the school team I had the privilege of watching them from full-back. Bez had a fantastic long spin pass, especially off his right hand, and we had a planned move from line-out ball off the top from our right, which simply involved him passing the ball direct to the outside centre. I know, because we used the same move when we were playing for 'Hoppers and sometimes I played in the centre and benefited from it, looping round from inside centre if the pass didn't quite reach the outside centre.

When he was in the mood, Bez would also try outrageous moves on a rugby pitch and would occasionally bring them off. The one that sticks in my mind was a try which he scored many years later in an away match at Wilmslow, which I think was for 'Hoppers third team. We had a line-out on the home team's 22, on our right-hand side, and I was waiting some distance away at fly-half for Bez's usual bullet pass. We won the ball and it was only when (in my mind) I was passing it to the centre that I realised that Bez had thrown the most outrageous dummy, which had also fooled all fourteen players in the line-out (and both hookers and the referee), all of whom were watching for the ball to go from me to the centre while Bez scooted round the front of the line-out and dotted the ball down without anyone laying a hand on him. I think he had already begun to saunter back towards the half-way line as if nothing special had occurred before anyone else realised what had actually happened.

With players like that in the school team, backed up by some keen and reasonably talented guys from my year (like the front row of Mike Thomas, Glen Leeming and Garry Whittle, and Hugh Metcalf – whom I have mentioned in chapter four – in the centre and myself at full-back), it was not surprising that we had a successful season in my last year at school and I for one enjoyed it. I guess that was also partly because my place in the team was secure, but another major factor for me was that I had got contact lenses at the beginning of that school year. Suddenly I could see everything more clearly when I was playing and I could judge the distance of the ball from me when it was in the air, which is vital when you are playing full-back. The difference it made for me was huge and it did wonders for my confidence as a player. It also made me begin to think that I could actually achieve something in the game after all, and that illusion was actually strengthened for a while when I arrived at university and did well in the freshers' trial match, but more of that later.

As you can probably imagine, Keith Aitchison was not my favourite person at that stage, simply because he was keeping me out of my favourite position, but it didn't take me long to realise that he was a far better player than I was, and he went on to have a glittering career, playing for Coventry, Warwickshire, Preston Grasshoppers, Fylde, Lancashire, England Students; and at the age of 18 for North West Counties against Australia. Keith also had an interview for a place at Durham and I looked after him when he came up, but nothing came of it and he ended up studying at Lanchester Polytechnic in Coventry, which is why he played rugby in that part of the world for a few years. Keith and I became good friends later on and we ended up playing a few games together towards the end of our careers, for the famous band of venerable gentlemen known as 'The Strollers', Preston Grasshoppers' veterans team. We have also accompanied each other on a few rugby trips in the last few years. Take a tip from me though (for reasons which you will understand when you read on), which is that if you ever go on tour with Keith you must at all costs do everything you possibly can to avoid having to room with him.

The Strollers team created many legends (and featured a few in successive team line-ups) in the period from 1979 to 2004, at the end of which those who were still playing (some of whom were by then in their late fifties or early sixties) decided to pack up at the same time, doing so with a final flourish, or 'Last Hurrah'. However, they didn't stop going on tour and that has continued ever since. The only difference is that the Strollers no longer play the game, but just go to watch and support.

Having been on some of the early trips, before I was a veteran, I'm pleased to say that I have been able to join in a few of the recent trips with my old mates (some of whom are now *very* old). In 2010 we flew to Treviso (which is near Venice) and watched

Treviso play Munster in the Heineken Cup. In 2011 we travelled by train all the way to Montpellier (well, most of us did; I actually had a little problem en route, as I shall explain later), and in 2012 we went by train again to La Rochelle to see their end-of-season match against Pau.

There is something really special about rugby purists (as we would like to think of ourselves) going abroad to watch a match in a different setting and culture and doing so as neutral spectators (although we tend to support the underdog, if there is one; we are Brits, after all). We are always made very welcome by the local rugby supporters and it is true that a kind of rugby brotherhood with the local rugby folk can be felt, but I guess what has made each of those trips really special for me is that I was spending a fun weekend with guys who played alongside me thirty or more years ago, and who are still comrades-in-arms (good mates) even though in some cases we have seen each other very little, if at all, in the intervening years.

One thing in particular made the Montpellier trip unforgettable for me. We had met up at Preston Station for an early train to London, had breakfast on the train (provided by ourselves) and were already having a very jolly time as we walked from Euston to the Eurostar terminal at St Pancras, where we met up with some of the Stroller exiles who live down south. Gathering up the refreshments we had brought with us for the journey, we made our way through security and on to passport control, where we all had to show our passports in order to be allowed through to board the train. I got mine out and saw to my horror that it wasn't mine at all, but my wife's! I was shown into the office of the man in charge (who was French, because the French immigration chaps run the operation at that point) and when I tried to explain the simple mistake I must have made and asked if I could get my wife to fax or e-mail a copy, there was no flexibility at all on offer from him and certainly no discernible evidence of a sense of humour (not even a flicker – I think he thought I was some kind of master criminal). Before I knew it I had been escorted back to the concourse and when I turned round he had disappeared and I was left there on my own. I texted my travelling companion, John Hicks, and said that I would have to go home for my passport and that I would see if I could get a flight to Montpellier, but that I didn't hold out much hope of success.

Back to Euston I went then, where I bought a ticket and managed to get on a train back to Preston more or less straight away. My wife Chris appeared quite sympathetic, but I think she did have a little chuckle to herself. She met me at the station and soon I was back at home, while my mates were still having a brilliant time, whizzing towards the south of France at enormous speed, without a care in the world. I fired up my computer and went on the internet, but although I discovered that there was an Easyjet flight direct to Montpellier the following morning it was from Gatwick, and the only flight I could find from the north was a scheduled flight from Leeds–Bradford for which the fare was over £500. I explained this to Chris and said that it wasn't worth bothering but, to her eternal credit, my wonderful wife then said that as I had really been looking forward to the trip I should go if I still wanted to do so and not worry about the cost. Fortunately, I was in a position to afford the substantial extra expense and with an offer like that I simply had to do it.

Back onto the internet I went and booked the flight from Gatwick early the next morning and an hotel room at Gatwick for that night. Chris took me back to the station for my third train journey of the day, back down to Euston this time. I walked to St Pancras, got a train to Gatwick, ate dinner alone in the hotel, got up at about 5.15 and caught the 6.30am flight. On arrival at Montpellier I took a taxi to the hotel and when I walked into reception (at about 10.30 local time, I think it was) who should be there but my old mate Martyn Hughes (still known to us all as 'Manuel', because in the seventies he used to do a passable impression of Andrew Sachs' Spanish waiter character Manuel in *Fawlty Towers*), who was one of the really good friends with whom I had played at 'Hoppers over thirty years previously. He explained that most of the guys had gone out looking for breakfast, so I dumped my gear and we went out looking for them. When we did locate them, seated en masse under the trees at an open-air café on a typically French boulevard, I'm sure you can imagine the ribbing I got, but I think I did also get a little respect from the guys for the effort I had made to catch up with them.

As it had turned out, I had missed very little of the weekend, and the rest of it was thoroughly enjoyable. However, apart from the extra cost of my little 'diversion' en route to Montpellier I did suffer two other penalties. The first was that because I was (obviously) the last to arrive I had no choice but to share a room with Keith Aitchison, who had joined the tour direct from a golfing holiday in France and so had been the last member of the party to arrive before I made my belated appearance. Keith is a nice chap (or so I thought), so the prospect of sharing a room with him didn't worry me at all – foolish naive boy that I still was at that stage – and I was in any event just happy to have made the trip after all. What I didn't realise was that that very evening Aitch would sneak back to the room and hide my passport (and yes, it really was mine this time). To be fair, Keith did (eventually) own up when I told him in the middle of the night that I couldn't find my passport, and he returned it to me in the morning. He *almost* apologised, but then he did at least have the decency to buy me breakfast.

The other snag was that as a result of my unplanned adventure I did acquire a new name, because I am now known as 'Christine' to all of the fraternity of Strollers, including those who weren't even on the tour!

Returning to my youth (Chris would say from my second childhood, but I don't think I ever left my first one; my very good friend John Hally says, *'Growing old is compulsory, but growing up is optional'*, and neither of us has any intention of doing the latter), rugby at school was fun, so I was determined to continue playing at university, and at club level. I still wanted to go as far as I could in the game and when I arrived at Durham I was very ambitious, hoping to make some progress. Although I became a reasonable club player, I was limited by a lack of basic talent (again) and by the fact that, even in those days, I really wasn't big enough. With the benefit of hindsight, although I played a reasonable amount of first-team club rugby I was really a second-team player. I was always keen and very determined, but I worked out later that I wasn't sufficiently skilful to be a top-level fly-half (I had seen what Aitch could do, after all); that at 10 stone 10lbs I wasn't really big enough to be a centre; that my kicking wasn't good enough for me to make it as a top-level full-back; and that my lack of real out-and-out speed meant that I would always have my limitations as a winger. I did play in all of those positions and I was probably an early version of what would now be called a 'utility back'. My position of choice was still fly-half, because I felt that I could usually use my wits to plot a way through the game and hopefully dictate the pattern of play to an extent, and I did get the chance to do that in the latter stages of my playing career, when I was playing lower down the teams.

Although I liked to play fly-half I wasn't really a goal-kicker, but I did sometimes perform that role and I once converted a try from the touchline. I remember that well! It was when I was at law college and was playing in an away match for one of the

Chester teams against a team in the Leigh area. As I lined up the kick the referee was standing next to me, so I asked him what was his favourite drink and told him that if the kick went over I would buy him a pint of it. To my amazement, it did.

That successful kick contrasts somewhat with a couple of others I can also remember. I was playing for Preston Grasshoppers first team away to Vale of Lune and when we drew level with a try in the last few minutes I had only to kick the conversion from more or less in front of the posts for us to win – I missed.

I also missed a penalty kick from in front of the posts in the final game of the season one year. It was during a game for Preston second team, away at Percy Park. I was at university at the time and had notched up 98 points for the season, including 20 tries (at 4 points each), so if I hadn't missed that final kick, that would have put me over 100 points for the only time in my playing career... DOH (again)!

As a player I used to consider myself a fly-half by choice and a centre by inclination. I was quite aggressive as a centre. I had to be, because I often found myself playing against centres who were two or three stones heavier than me. I did enjoy the confrontational element of it, and my lack of size made it all the more satisfying when I did manage to bring a big guy crashing down to earth. Being smaller also meant that I could be quite elusive, and if they wanted to flatten me the big guys had to catch me first (but quite a few did, of course!). The one thing I could (usually) do quite well was to tackle, but again I didn't have a lot of choice because when I got into the first team at Preston we were a pretty poor team. I didn't play many games in my first year in the team, because I was away at university for much of the season, so it wasn't *all* my fault, but I think that was the season when the first team won only four times in the whole of the season. We had to do a lot of defending, which was tough, but it did mean that I appreciated it all the more when I played in more successful teams. It's all about perspective, isn't it?

Despite my limitations I enjoyed my rugby immensely and I played a lot of games at all levels over a long period. I played with and against some very good players, including a few (then) current and former internationals. I went on tours to various parts of the world and I got to know some great guys, a good number of whom are still friends to this day. Despite the aches and pains I feel now as an older guy (and especially the two worn discs in my lumbar spine) I wouldn't have missed a moment of it.

With some of my old rugby mates at Hoppers, Sept 2013. Jim Martin is to my left and Dick Greenwood is in front of me.

Off to Durham I went in October 1972, quite full of myself and thinking that, now that my contact lenses enabled me to see properly on the pitch, I might actually make it as a player or at least work my way into the university first team (which I did manage for two games, but only in my final year). The difficulty was that the standard at Durham was incredibly high, as was highlighted by the fact that every year one or two schoolboy internationals and a number of schoolboy county players would go up as freshers and obviously I was neither of those. However, I did discover some years later that Bob Reeves, an ex 'Hopper who at the time was the coach of the UAU (Universities Athletic Union) team and who I believe is now a high-ranking official at the RFU (Rugby Football Union), had apparently sent word to the rugby people at Durham suggesting that they should look out for me, seemingly because he had been watching me in training at 'Hoppers and was impressed by my handling and distribution as a fly-half/centre. Thinking about it now, though, it is possible that someone may have been winding me up because if Bob did watch me in training it can't have been before my second year at Durham, as I didn't play for 'Hoppers at all before Christmas 1972, after the end of my first term at Durham. It's still a nice thought that someone as knowledgeable about rugby as Bob might just have said complimentary things about me. I wish I had known it at the time, though, because if I had I would definitely have stuck to playing fly-half or centre.

As it was, having had some success as a full-back at school I had decided that that was the position for me and I played there in the freshers' trials. I think I attempted the old trick of wearing odd-coloured socks in the hope that that might improve my chances of being noticed by the selectors, but I was aware that I genuinely played quite well that day. Imagine my astonishment and pride when I was selected to play for the University second team in the first match of term. Perhaps I was going to make some kind of breakthrough after all. To be fair, I was told that the regular full-back was injured and I was warned that I probably wouldn't be in the second team the next week. That didn't matter to me, because at least I was being given a chance to prove my worth. Sadly, that was as far as it went, because I played poorly and my kicking let me down badly. The situation got worse quite quickly, because the following week I was crestfallen to discover that I hadn't just been dropped – I hadn't even been selected for any of the university's four teams.

I decided to cut my losses and that I wouldn't try to play for any of the university teams that year, but would play just for the college team instead, on Wednesdays. I enjoyed that and I played pretty well at that level for the rest of that season, scoring quite a lot of points in the process. I resumed university rugby in my second year, playing mainly for the third or fourth team, although I think I may have had the odd game for the second team. That year I often found myself playing with an open-side flanker called Mark McDowell (nickname Billy Big Bum, would you believe), who only the year before had played in the England Schools' team with Aitch. That was in the university third team, which just shows how high the standard was at Durham.

Both university and college rugby that year were a lot of fun. We were incredibly fit and I was one of those who had returned to Durham two weeks early so we could take part in pre-term fitness training. We trained twice a day for ten days in succession

Grey College, Durham rugby team 1972-73. I'm the one on the back row with the Kevin Keegan haircut.

and for some of the sessions we were taken by minibus to the coast so we could run up and down the sand dunes. We were also very quick on the field of play, invariably far quicker than most of the club third and fourth teams who were our opposition most weeks, and certainly both quicker and better than just about all the other university teams we encountered. We played open, attacking rugby as much as we could and as a result we scored countless tries.

I remember playing for the university third team against York University second team and beating them 108–0 (and back then a try was worth only 4 points), and scoring 4 tries and 6 conversions myself in a big victory for the university fourth team against Darlington Mowden Park fourth team. Basically, we knew that we were going to win virtually all of our matches, even though the forwards in some of the club teams we met were of far bigger build (and much more experienced) than our forwards.

They were happy days indeed, and even though I was playing lower down the university teams it did a lot for my confidence as a player. I played as much as I could throughout the season, which for university students meant the winter and spring terms. It may have been in my third year, but I did once play in nine matches in 14 days, including two in the same day. I think there was an inter-colleges cup match one Saturday morning, and then I got called into one of the university teams in the afternoon. On top of that I was also training twice a week, so I think you will understand just how fit I was – I just wish I had been at least two stones heavier, that's all!

The college team was also quite successful, particularly in my last year. A very good centre had come to Durham and to Grey College, from my old school. His name was Dave Stevens and he was studying engineering on an Army scholarship. In due course he gained a First and went on to become a career soldier in the Royal Engineers. The last I heard he was a brigadier, but I guess he will have retired by now. Dave was a top-class centre who became a regular in the university first team, but for me it was a great joy to play with him on Wednesdays in the Grey team. We had a handy guy at fly-half, so I played outside centre with Dave at inside centre. He created lots of space for me, and I ran in quite a few tries as a result. I can remember one of them as if it had happened yesterday – I know, sad, isn't it?

I became a regular in the university second team in my last year and I still have the team photo as proof. I played at centre again and my regular centre partner was Marcus Wyburn Mason (you wouldn't forget a name like that, would you?). That was also a very good team and the team photo reminds me that our playing record was P21 W17 D1 L3 – not bad, eh?

Durham University 2nd XV, 1974-75. Not a bad record eh?

I played for the first team twice that season, both times on the wing, but only once on merit. The first time was at the end of pre-term training, before term proper started and crucially before the freshers had arrived. That meant that there was a shortage of players for the first match, so I was selected to play on the right wing, against Darlington. Unfortunately, my lack of real pace caught me out as the opposition's left wing was at least two yards quicker than me and he ended up scoring a hat trick of tries – oops!

Naturally, I imagined that that would be my one-and-only appearance for Durham University first team, but I was wrong. Later in the season I was picked to play in an away match against Wigton in Cumbria, again on the right wing. I had played for the fourth, third and second teams in succession over the previous three weeks (scoring at least one try in each of those matches), so being selected for the first team completed what may well have been a unique achievement.

I played quite well that day (although I didn't get picked again) and I really enjoyed the experience of being involved in a good team alongside some classy players, including several who were full county players (in the days when the County Championship was still a big deal). My main memory of the day was when I came off my wing with perfect timing to execute a crash tackle on the opposing outside centre, just as he was about to go outside the centre inside me. A success for a 150lb weakling, don't you think?

So much for my rugby career at university – now for my time as a club player.

I first played for Preston Grasshoppers RFC in December 1972, after my first term at university. When I arrived home that December I rang the club secretary, George Thompson, and told him I would like to play. When he asked which teams I had played for, I told him (truthfully) Kirkham Grammar School and Durham University second team. Fortunately, he didn't ask how many games I had played for the university second team. I ended up playing a few games for 'Hoppers over that Christmas period and then a few more during the Easter vacation. I can't remember which team I played for, but it was probably the third or possibly second team, I think. One of the guys I played with bore the memorable name of Ellis Wilkinson, a name I was already familiar with because he came from a well-known Preston family who were manufacturers of mineral waters, and as a child I had derived great pleasure from drinking their legendary brew known as 'Ellis Wilkinson's Dandelion and Burdock'. For many years I had wondered what became of Ellis, and then he introduced himself to me after a game at 'Hoppers at Christmas 2012!

In 1972, the club was still at its old ground at Lea which was definitely very tired and run down. I remember in particular that the concrete bottom of the communal bath was very rough on the skin! Fortunately, the ground was about to be sold for housing development, and in summer 1973 we all moved to the club's present home at Lightfoot Green.

I think it was before the move, probably at Easter 1973, that I went on my first 'overseas' rugby tour, a second-team tour to the Isle of Man! I could be wrong, but that was probably when I first got to know guys like Dave Nichols ('Snowy'), Gary Miller and Martin Hothersall, with whom I played for many years after that. Incredibly, I bumped into Gary at a quiz in a local pub only a few days before writing this, not having seen him for about thirty years. We flew from Blackpool, which was another first for me (flying, I mean, not Blackpool), in a rickety and very noisy old prop-driven plane, a Handley Page Herald I believe.

Over that summer and even when the season started, the facilities were very basic, simply because the building work on the clubhouse hadn't been finished. Initially there were no baths or showers, just a cold-water tap. However, a much worse problem was that the grounds had previously been the site of Will Bradley's Duck Farm. The new pitches were poorly drained and they soon became a stinking morass, the smell of which made all too obvious the all-pervading presence of significant quantities of duck manure (to put it politely). It was very unpleasant and quite a few of the players, including myself, ended up with impetigo (a nasty skin infection) and I still have the scars on my shins as evidence.

As I have said, the club didn't have much playing strength then, and when the 1973–74 season began I was soon pressing for a place in the first team, or certainly when I arrived home from Durham that Christmas. I made my debut against Blackburn on New Year's Day 1974, aged nineteen. Yes, we did have matches on New Year's Day then, and on Boxing Day as well!

I played at full-back. I can't remember the names of the rest of the team, but I know that John Grimbaldeston ('Grim') was in the centre and I'm sure that Keith Brierley ('Dad') *must* have been on the right wing. Keith was certainly a first-team star then and he was the one veteran who didn't stop playing when the rest of the Strollers did. He finally retired from playing on 20th April 2013, and I'm pleased to say that I was able to be there to watch, along with a whole host of my old playing pals. Keith was 71 at the time and had completed 52 consecutive seasons playing for the club! Not a bad record, old lad.

I did play in the first team a few more times that season, including going on my first first-team tour, but the problem for me, and for the other students who were away at university for much of the season, was that every time I came home I had to start again trying to win back my place in the first team, and I didn't always succeed. In an effort to compensate for that the club did organise a students' team one year. I was in that team. We played together only a handful of times, but there were some very good players in the team, and it was good fun.

In those days, the club had an Easter tour every year which tended to rotate between South Wales, Cornwall and Gloucestershire (Forest of Dean, that sort of area). The tour in 1974 was to South Wales and I played in all three games, all of which we lost. We played Maesteg under lights (a new experience for me) in front of fairly full stands on the Friday night, Tredegar on Saturday afternoon and Penarth on Monday morning. It was a completely crazy schedule, but we still enjoyed the trip (up to a point). I was playing in the centre and I struggled a bit because, the Saturday before the tour, I had played for the first team away at Wakefield (who were a top team then) and had suffered bruised ribs in a very physical game.

Maesteg were clearly a better team than us, but they still chose to engage in all sorts of off-the-ball skulduggery (cheap shots on the blind side of the referee and so on), egged on by a very partisan crowd who cheered every punch. I haven't been too keen on Welsh club sides ever since, but I did get sweet revenge some years later. A junior Welsh club side came to the North West on tour one Easter and one of their games was at Preston against our third team, for which I was playing. We got the distinct impression that they weren't too impressed at being asked to play our third team and we weren't surprised when they adopted the familiar Welsh tactic of trying to cheat and punch their way to victory. What they didn't realise was that we had a very good third team at the time (skippered by Gregg Butler) which included a number of players who had performed at a pretty decent level. Not only did we stand up to their violence, but we also ran them off their feet and hammered them with a really good display of attacking rugby, on what I recall was a hot and sunny day. A happy day indeed!

I joined three more first-team tours in the following years, two to Cornwall and one to the West Country. The rugby was pretty intense, but a good time was had by all.

Touring for 'Hoppers entered a new era when we went on our first real overseas tour in 1978, to the Cayman Islands and Miami, no less. It was a completely new experience for me, my first proper overseas trip of any kind, first time in the USA and my first time trying to play rugby in subtropical conditions as well. The tour began on 4th May 1978 and that was quite a week for me because I had been admitted to the Roll of Solicitors three days earlier, on Monday 1st May. I had no money, but a very far-sighted manager at Midland Bank must have decided that I was a safe bet, because he agreed to lend me the £200 which I needed for tour spending money. I still remember his name: Eric Lake (thank you, Eric!).

My old friend Jim Martin was playing for 'Hoppers by then, so we stayed together on Grand Cayman. The whole tour party were guests in the homes of players and club officials from the Cayman team and Jim and I were 'billeted' with a lovely couple called Dave and Anita Wheaton, from whom I still receive a Christmas card every year. It was certainly no hardship, as they had a huge bungalow just outside the capital, George Town, complete with a maid who had instructions to feed us when Dave and Anita were out. The bungalow was only fifty yards from Seven Mile Beach on the island's west coast. This looked just like everyone's idea of a beach in a tropical paradise (remember the Bounty adverts on TV?) because that is exactly what it was.

Jim is a year older than me and after he went up to Newcastle University to read Latin (no, I didn't understand that either), our paths crossed only occasionally over the next few years. After Newcastle he went to London where he trained and qualified as a chartered surveyor. He then secured a job back in Preston and so got back in touch. He had continued to play football to a fairly good amateur level while he was living in London, but he told me when he came home that he had grown tired of the attitude of most footballers, and of the lack of a good social side to that game. However, his employers in London had asked him to play for them in a seven-a-side rugby tournament and when he did so he had found that he had enjoyed his first experience of any kind of rugby, and of course the social side to boot! As a result Jim had decided by the time he returned to Preston that he would give

Playing on the wing on my first overseas rugby tour in 1978, in the Cayman Islands –
it was very hot!

rugby proper a go. I tried to help and encourage him as much as I could. The outcome was that (because of his raw talent and not as a result of any help I gave him) Jim was playing full-back for the first team within about eighteen months, at a time when I was struggling to get into the team myself!

Not having had a rugby upbringing, Jim was an unorthodox player, even naive sometimes, and he was a big success in the first team for a couple of years or so. Surprisingly for someone who had been a good footballer, Jim didn't actually kick very well, but he was a very strong tackler and an excellent counter-attacking runner. Sadly, Jim's rugby career was short-lived, effectively brought to an end by a back injury that ultimately required surgery. We were on tour in the South of France in 1979 and were warming up in the changing room before our second game. Jim was running on the spot when he suddenly stopped and grabbed his back. That was effectively it for Jim, although he did play for a few more years and was on our next big overseas tour, which was to Canada in 1982. How tough it was to be an amateur rugby player in those days!

Happily, Jim and I are now playing sport together again on a fairly regular basis. I have been playing golf since I was thirty-five, but Jim took it up only after he retired from work at the age of fifty-five. That means that he has some catching up to do, but typically Jim is determined to master the infuriating game that is golf.

I continued to go on tour with 'Hoppers for a few years after that, and our next big overseas tour was the aforementioned one to Canada in 1982. I helped to organise that and arranged much of the fundraising ahead of the trip. We played the first match near Toronto, then travelled by bus to Ottawa for two more games, then back to Toronto for a fourth. As with the Cayman tour we were hosted by the families of the guys we played against, and that offered us an insight into the people as well as the places we visited. Ottawa in particular was a lovely small city – I recommend anyone to visit.

I wasn't selected for the first game (which we lost) but played in the other three (which we won, but I don't think there was any direct correlation between those two facts). Once again, I have some happy memories of that tour, especially when I look at my photo album and see the faces of my fellow tourists, some of whom are no longer with us. The truth is that at that stage of my professional career I simply would not have been able to afford to fly to such far-flung and exotic places had it not been for the rugby tours, even if I had had the initiative to organise such trips for myself, but apart from that there is nothing quite like being a member of a close-knit group of guys determined to play good rugby and to have a good time in the process.

One notable point about the tour to Canada was that we had in the party an up-and-coming young second-row by the name of Wade Dooley, who made quite an impact on the trip (and on any opposing players who got in his way). At 6 foot 8 inches and weighing in at 18 stone, Wade was some physical specimen and it was about three years later that he made his debut for England, going on to become one of the best second-rows ever to play for England and the British and Irish Lions. Wade was (and is) a nice guy but he didn't take any prisoners on the pitch and it was always enjoyable to be on his team rather than opposing him!

Towards the end of my time in 'Hoppers first-team squad, which came in about 1982 or 1983 I think, we were coached for a couple of seasons by Dick Greenwood, past England captain and father of Will Greenwood, 2003 World Cup winner and now Sky TV pundit. Dick was a real character and a good coach who went on to coach England for a while. He played for 'Hoppers for a couple of years and although he would have been in his late

Team photo on tour in Canada, 1982. The big guy on the back row is Wade Dooley, later of England and the Lions.

thirties by then he was still a tremendously talented and successful number 8, especially when working with his partner-in-crime Brian Ashton, who had also toured with England (at scrum-half), and who of course also later coached England. I did play in one or two games with both of them, which was a tremendous privilege and education.

Inevitably, I began to slide down the teams as better players came on the scene – or players the selectors thought were better than me; I didn't always agree, but I rarely voiced those feelings. By then I was aware I was really a second-team standard player who had been fortunate to have played quite a few games in the first team (when it wasn't very good). There were times when I was actually better than the player who was taking my position in the first team, but somehow it didn't get noticed, and as I had been around the club a long time by then I began to wonder if it was a case of familiarity breeding contempt. There was one particular first-team captain who clearly didn't rate me as a player, but one

Preston Grasshoppers 1st team, Sept 1980. I was on the bench that day.

year he had no choice but to select me as full-back in the last game of the season. I happened to score a solo try from about sixty yards out and as we were trotting back to the half-way line he actually said to me, 'I didn't know you could do that.' I have since thought that that said a lot more about him than it did about me.

I also once played in a pre-season trial match opposite a then incumbent first-team centre. I outplayed him and he never got past me once (though he did try a few times), but he was still selected ahead of me. I realised then that my time in the team was up and, rather than kick my heels in the second team and perhaps block a place that could have been taken up by an aspiring first-teamer, I moved down to the third team, where I became a regular for a couple of really enjoyable seasons. When Dick Greenwood was coaching at the club, I offered to captain the third team the following season, thinking that I could perhaps help bring on some of the younger players. That was the last I heard of it, and not only was I not asked, but no one bothered to tell me that, let alone explain why they thought I was not the right man for that job.

In 1983 I decided to follow Martyn Hughes to another club. He was an old mate with whom I had played in the first team and he had agreed to take up the captaincy of Chorley, a smaller club which played at a much lower level than 'Hoppers. I had concluded that if I went with Martyn I ought to have a chance of playing some first-team rugby for a year or two, but the plan didn't work out, or at least not in the 1983–84 season. I tore a knee cartilage in a pre-season trial match and when it was confirmed that I would need an operation I decided to put that off until the following spring, because I was getting married in December that year. I had the operation the following February and I did then play one full season for Chorley in 1984–85. I enjoyed that season, playing fly-half or centre, usually alongside Brian Eagle, who became quite a good friend.

I was thirty by then. After that I went back to 'Hoppers for the rest of my playing career, playing in the fourth team with a good bunch of guys (and winning more often than not). However, I think my age and relatively small stature were starting to take their toll, and I began to pick up more and more injuries. I decided to retire when I was thirty-three, but I did play about six more games three years later before retiring for a second time, again because of injuries.

My third and final retirement came after a full season playing for the Strollers – 'Hoppers aforementioned band of venerable gentlemen (veterans' team) – in 1994–95. Just before the end of the previous season I had gone to the club to watch a first-team match, as a guest of the sponsors. We were about to go into lunch when I came across some of my old mates from the Strollers, who were about to set off to play in Yorkshire that afternoon. They were a man short – so you can probably guess what happened next. I think it was Max Horton who asked me if I had my boots with me. I said, 'No, but I know where they are', and was soon being driven the half-mile to my house to retrieve them from the loft!

I was completely unfit, not having played rugby for about four years, but amazingly all the old feelings and enthusiasm returned when I got onto the pitch, although the first tackle took a bit of courage, which I managed to summon up from somewhere. I played on the wing and really enjoyed it. Perhaps inevitably, I scored a try, which meant I was hooked again, so I made myself available to play the following season (with my wife's permission, of course). I enjoyed that season enormously, playing in a good team with some great guys, some of whom had played at a very good level in their time, including Aitch; and Wade also played the odd game. After the end of the season I went on the Strollers' annual tour to Belgium in May 1995. We stayed in Mechelen (what a lovely place that was) and I played my last ever match against Dendermonde. I played on the wing and the last thing I did was to score a try, so it wasn't a bad way to go out, except that I broke my wrist in the process! Strangely, although I had suffered numerous injuries playing rugby over the years, that was the first and only time I broke a bone.

The pass for that try was given to me by John Heritage ('J.H.'). He was a Preston lad who, as a young man, had turned professional and in his rugby league career played for Warrington, Barrow and Blackpool Borough. He was a centre (and a good one at that), but he once told me that the first time he played against Wigan at Central Park he was put on the wing, so he was marking the legendary Billy Boston, one of the all-time greats of rugby league. In other words, the guy who gave me my last pass on a rugby pitch had played in direct opposition to Billy Boston. That will do for me!

If I could have done so, I probably would have carried on playing for the Strollers for a few more years. The Strollers managed another nine years as a team, and some of them were several years older than me, but continuing with them wasn't to happen for me, because about a month after we got back from Belgium I slipped a disc, and I knew immediately that that was the end of playing rugby for me.

Rugby career over, I wondered what I should do next in terms of sporting activity. I started watching rugby and still do that (I am a regular at 'Hoppers these days and I go to at least one international match every year, usually taking my son Andy with me), but I was only forty-one and not the kind of guy to remain inactive, in spite of my now fragile back. The answer was golf, and with sensible management my back hasn't hampered me too much. I had already dabbled with social golf in my mid-thirties, having joined Preston Golf Club in 1989, but now I decided to take it a little more seriously.

I will mention something of my golfing exploits later, but first I want to tell you about a spot of extreme hill-walking I did in 1999, when I was forty-five years old. I climbed Kilimanjaro, the highest mountain in Africa at 19,340 feet. Physically, it was without doubt the most difficult thing I have ever done, but also the most rewarding and genuinely a once-in-a-lifetime experience. The trek came about through Saltmine Trust, the Christian charity based in Dudley in the West Midlands which was originally established as the support mechanism for a Dudley lad named Dave Pope, gospel singer and evangelist. Saltmine was also working in the area of Christian arts, especially theatre, and in supporting various projects in developing countries through its 'Trailblazers' division. I had already been a long-term supporter of Saltmine, but by 1999 I was also a trustee of the charity. The main aim of the trip was to raise funds for various development projects in Africa, through sponsorship of the team members, which we each had to raise ourselves. We also all paid all our own fares and other expenses, so that meant that we could assure sponsors that none of the money which they donated would be used to pay any of the costs of sending us there.

We achieved our objectives, the first of which was to get all twenty of our party to the rim of the crater, which counts as having climbed the mountain even if you don't then walk the extra half-mile or so to reach the very highest point (which is called Uhuru Point – good quiz question, that). We were a mixed bunch from all over the country, but we got on well and certainly pulled together when that was required. The second objective was of course to raise as much money as possible – between us we raised over £70,000. Remember, this was 1999.

I won't bore you now with all the minute detail of the expedition (I suspect that I have already done that to far too many people since 1999). I did keep a journal during the trip and if anyone is really interested I can make it available for them to read. When I read through it again myself recently, it did make surprisingly interesting reading (for me anyway) and it reminded me just how demanding the trek had been.

At about 15,000 feet on the way up Kilimanjaro, Tanzania in 1999. Joe Cool or what?

I wrote an article for our church magazine about my 'Kili' adventure and this is what I said about the day we actually reached the summit:

> *'How do you describe such a day? Physically, the*
> *hardest day of my life, by far, but we did it. We were*
> *on the go for over 17 hours and walking for over 14*
> *of those. We climbed over 3,000 feet, starting at just*
> *over 16,000 feet in a temperature of -5 centigrade and*
> *descended 7,500 feet.'*

In my usual fashion I had been determined to train hard before we went, in order to get as fit as I could. I decided that the best way to do that would be to do lots of walking, especially in the hills. I started the previous autumn, walking on the flat initially, for example from Preston to Garstang along the canal towpath, and then in the hills, gradually going higher and further and more often throughout that winter. I did walk with others sometimes, but I usually went out walking on my own, particularly in the Lakeland fells. It gave me the perfect excuse to revive my love of fell-walking, and over the course of a few months I managed to 'bag' quite a few of the 'Wainwrights' for the first time. I would set off very early on those winter mornings so I could be up in the Lake District and out on the fells soon after it had come light. The high point was when I did the 'Newlands Round', walking fifteen miles with over 5,000 feet of ascent and returning to my car by about 1.30pm.

Ascending Kilimanjaro was tough for sure, but I'm really glad I did it. The main problem was the effects of altitude, but despite that, anyone who is reasonably fit can succeed, provided they are prepared to do some training in advance and to follow to the letter the instructions which are given by the local guides during the trek itself. So if you are fit enough and you get the chance to climb Kili, go for it!

I have included my Kili adventure in this chapter because it was a physical challenge more than anything else and therefore (in my eyes) definitely part of my sporting career.

These days I play golf as much as I reasonably can, but I also watch a lot of sport, both live and on TV. I don't attend many football matches nowadays or even watch much football on TV. Frankly I find the Premier League matches boring, and when I do watch them on TV they usually send me to sleep – or is that just caused by my age? I still follow Preston North End, but I haven't been to a match at Deepdale for quite a while.

As well as playing golf I like to watch it when I can. I have been to the Open Championship many times over the years, but my best ever experience watching golf was when I went with my old rugby pal John Hicks to the Ryder Cup at Medinah near Chicago at the end of September 2012. It was an expensive package tour, but it was worth every penny. It would have been an incredible experience even without Europe's amazing comeback win on the final day and I consider myself very fortunate to have been able to witness it live. Watching any sport on TV simply does not compare with the experience of being there in person, soaking up the atmosphere. If I get the chance one day, I would still like to go on a British Lions rugby tour, and possibly even an England cricket tour to the West Indies. Who knows?

If I were to describe myself as a golfer I would probably say, 'Very keen, tries hard, but not very good'. Having said that, the beauty of the golf handicap system is that, even though I am a very average golfer, I can still win prizes from time to time and I once won a club competition (a few years ago now, mind). I would hope to carry on playing for a good few more years yet, as long as

I can still enjoy it, but I don't intend to carry on beyond the point at which physical frailty starts to get the better of me. After that, there is always Crown Green bowling, and I do still have my dad's woods!

At the Ryder Cup at Medinah, Chicago 2012. As you can see from my face it was very hot.

CHAPTER ELEVEN

HEROES
My heroes and why they make the list

Sir Tom Finney

The gentleman who was Sir Tom just had to be on my list, given that I am a proud Prestonian. The motto of the 2012 London Olympics was 'Inspire a Generation' and Tom did that in the forties, fifties and sixties. There must have been countless little boys throughout England and beyond, but especially in Preston, who were inspired by him to kick a ball in the first place, but then to try to do it better.

Sadly, I was just too young to have seen Tom play. The first Preston North End game I attended was in 1963, a couple of years after he had retired (they lost, but they did have a good team and football historians will tell you that the following year, in 1964, they reached the FA Cup Final as a second-tier team). It went downhill from that point, and as I said at my dad's funeral in 2012, I learned very early on that if you are going to support Preston North End it will *always* end in tears.

It was on my tenth birthday in 1964 that dad took me to the FA Cup semi-final at Villa Park in Birmingham. We travelled by coach and I can picture the scene now. Preston beat Swansea 2–1 and Preston's centre-half Tony Singleton scored the winner with what was probably the only goal of his entire career, when he returned a clearance with interest, hoofing it all the way from the centre circle and over the goalkeeper's head into the net. I didn't go to the final at Wembley, which is probably just as well because Preston were beaten 3–2 by a West Ham team which included three guys who were to star in England's World Cup winning team two years later: Bobby Moore, Geoff Hurst and Martin Peters. They were still very lucky to come back from a 2–1 deficit at half-time, though, and I maintain to this day that Preston would have won if substitutes had been allowed in those days. Preston's star goalie, Alan Kelly, hurt his back and could hardly move when West Ham scored their second and third goals. Not that I'm at all bitter, of course!

I can still remember Preston's cup final team: Kelly, Ross, Smith, Lawton, Singleton, Kendall, Wilson, Ashworth, Dawson, Spavin and Holden!

Around that time a sales rep for a local animal feed firm, Bambers, who was a regular visitor to our farm, gave me a football book which I still have today. I think his name was Sam Wignall. The book was entitled *Instructions to Young Footballers* and it was written by Tom Finney himself. It is a very practical explanation, with illustrations, about how to kick with either foot, head a ball, trap, tackle, shoot and dribble, and also how to get and stay fit. I followed it avidly and spent hours in the farmyard practising these skills, particularly kicking with my left foot (I am naturally right-handed and right-footed). Tom was left-footed, but he played on both wings for Preston and England, as well as at centre-forward. Like Tom, when I did later

play in teams I often found myself playing on the 'wrong' wing, in my case the left, but I hasten to add, that turned out to be the solitary similarity between us as players!

Sir Tom was incredibly talented, versatile, hard-working and loyal, and – above all – humble. I have met him a few times and for a year or two I was secretary of a sporting trust in Preston of which Tom was a trustee (as was the former Lancashire and West Indies cricketer Clive Lloyd – what a nice man he was, and what a big guy; I don't think I have ever seen anyone with hands anything like as big as his!). Sir Tom was gracious and helpful, and just a lovely man.

Anyone to whom I have spoken who saw Tom play has said that he was the best player they ever watched. The former Liverpool manager, the late great Bill Shankly, played with Tom at Preston and his description of Tom as a player probably summed him up best. About the time George Best was at his peak as a player, someone apparently asked Bill if Best was as good as Finney. He thought about it for a moment, then replied in his distinctive Scots accent, 'Aye, I suppose you would say he is – but you must remember that Tom is sixty-five.'

The book I mentioned above had been autographed not just by Tom himself, but also by the rest of the Preston team in about 1958, when they were still one of the best teams in the country. Those who signed included Bill Shankly, but also other notable players like Tommy Docherty and Willie Cunningham, the Preston captain for a long time, who for many years after his retirement had a sports shop in Church Street in Preston. I once showed the book to Tom at a sports trust meeting, and he was kind enough to sign it again, this time for my son Andy. I guess the book will be quite valuable now, and I did at one time think of donating it to the National Football Museum when it was still located at Preston's ground, Deepdale, but I will certainly not do that now that the museum has been moved to join the footballing millionaires in Manchester. I will probably give it to Andy one day, or leave it to him in my will.

Barry John

Barry John was another sporting hero from my youth. At the age of seventeen I was spellbound when I watched footage of the 1971 British and Irish Lions rugby tour of New Zealand, of which Barry John was the star among a host of stars in that very special team. He had a unique talent and had not just the skill to do things on a rugby pitch that others wouldn't even contemplate, but also the sheer audacity to try them in the first place. To this day, when archive films of some of the matches on that tour are shown on TV, they still make my skin tingle.

Of course, Barry played in the amateur era, and I remember thinking when he retired at the age of 27 that it was far too early for him to stop playing. He was at the very peak of his career, and I guess he thought that having achieved all he had ever wanted in the game, where else would he go, but with the benefit of hindsight I admire him for having opted out when he did. I have heard him say only recently that he had to put his family and career first, given that he was not allowed to be paid for playing rugby. It clearly would have been a different case if he had been playing in the professional era, but if he had, I'm not convinced that he would be remembered quite so fondly as is the case now.

He did inspire me. As a teenager I wanted to be a fly-half, just like Barry John. I did achieve that, but to be truthful I had my limitations, as I have explained in chapter ten. However, there was one day which is still clear in my mind when something special did happen. I was at university at the time and had spent the morning before a Saturday afternoon match reading Barry's autobiography. Before the game I felt really good. I was really fit and confident in my own ability and I definitely felt inspired by what I had read from the great man. I simply knew that I would play well that day and for once it actually happened. I went into the match determined to go for it, to try things I might not normally attempt and to try to boss the game. I did all of those things and probably never played better in my life.

I'm sure things were back to normal in the next match, but did that matter? No, of course it didn't and at least I had the memory of that one very special day.

Others have summed up Barry John's unique qualities as a player in ways far more eloquent than mine, particularly some of the other great players who played with him. I will quote two of them, Gareth Edwards, and Gerald Davies.

Gareth Edwards said of Barry: '*He had this marvellous easiness in the mind, reducing problems to their simplest form, backing his own talent all the time. One success on the field bred another and soon he gave off a cool superiority which spread to others in the side.*'

That definitely could never have been said of me as a player (I wish!).

Gerald Davies said that while Gareth Edwards was fiery and impulsive, B.J. was, '*fairer, aloof and apart. While the hustle and bustle went on around him he could divorce himself from it all: he kept his emotions in check and a careful rein on the surrounding action. The game would go according to his will and no one else's.*'

George Best had that X factor when he played football, but he doesn't appear in my list of heroes because of his lifestyle. The same applies to Tiger Woods, but by way of contrast the great American golfer Tom Watson has come very close, mainly because of his sportsmanship and consistently pleasant demeanour.

Sheila Etherington OBE

Most of you probably won't have heard of Sheila, but she is a real-life heroine. She's a couple of years older than me and I first knew her as the only girl in the family on the next-door farm, the one we had to pass on the lane down to Newsham Lodge. Her family were staunch Methodists and I remember my parents thinking that they were a bit extreme because they steadfastly refused to do any unnecessary work on Sundays, to the extent that they wouldn't make hay on a Sunday, even if it was the only day for weeks when the weather was right for the job.

When I started school at the age of four I had to walk there (it was exactly a mile from our yard to the village school) with my two older sisters and Sheila and her two brothers, and Sheila has since told me that her memory of me at that stage was that I would take great delight in collecting worms and snails and the like along the way and presenting them to her, as though I was giving her something special. Charming lad, eh?

When Sheila grew up she became a nurse and then a midwife, but she always felt called to overseas mission and in 1983 she was appointed by the Free Methodist Church to be a missionary nurse at Kibogora Hospital on the shores of Lake Kivu in western Rwanda, in central Africa. Initially a nurse administrator, she has since done just about every job in the hospital, from administration and nurse training to being a health visitor. She was there when the genocide happened in 1994 and she escaped with her life only because she was whisked away at the last minute by the US Marines. The hospital was looted and many of Sheila's staff were killed and she still won't talk about some of the things that happened in that truly awful period. But you know what? Sheila couldn't wait to go back, and she was the first expat to do just that, as soon as it was deemed safe. She then set about establishing projects to help provide meaningful employment for teenage boys and girls who had been orphaned in the genocide, many of whom had since fallen into crime or prostitution.

Sheila's role has changed significantly as she approaches retirement and more Rwandan folk are now involved in the running of the hospital, and indeed the university which has recently been established there, but at the time of writing she is still there. Sheila has always been publicity shy, not a fan of the spotlight in any way (and I mean, she *really* doesn't like it), but in 2008 she had no choice when she was appointed OBE in the New Year's Honours list, and she was even persuaded to attend the investiture by Her Majesty the Queen at Buckingham Palace (but only because she didn't want to disappoint her very proud parents).

If ever an honour was richly deserved, that was it, although if it had been up to me she would now be known as Dame Sheila Etherington, something I can say with confidence she would certainly have disliked immensely![1]

CHAPTER TWELVE

CLOSING THOUGHTS
Regrets, thank-yous and what's next

The time has come for some concluding remarks. If you have turned first to the last chapter of this book in order to find how this particular story ends – shame on you! It's not a novel, you know, and in any case I'm pleased to say that my story hasn't quite finished yet, thank you very much.

First, to share a few regrets. I am not the kind of person to worry about things, or to dwell on mistakes, but I have learned that it does no harm to look back occasionally on mistakes or omissions in the obvious hope of finding ways of avoiding repeating them. After a round of golf (perhaps the next day) it's always a good idea to think back through the bad shots and the wrong club selections and so on, to try to establish what went wrong and why, and also to think how the good shots might be repeated more often. It's a truism, I know, but in life we do tend to learn more from our mistakes than from our successes.

What I do regret are the mistakes I have made which in one way or another have impacted on clients, or have led to them being disappointed with the level of service provided. Fortunately, in nearly forty years in the law, I have had very few such problems, but it would be unrealistic to pretend that they never happened, although I still wish they hadn't.

I also wish to express my heartfelt gratitude to the large number of people who have helped and supported me in different ways. I mentioned in chapter seven some of those who have provided particular support in my professional career, but personal thanks are also due to a variety of other folk and I will name a few here:

Geoff Parkinson

For having the vision to start a Pathfinder Group in Woodplumpton, and the courage to see it through (see chapter two).

Barrie Walton

The founding pastor of Fulwood Free Methodist Church, the church which I have now attended for over 30 years, for his wise counsel and support in the early years in particular; and also for being such a help to my wife following the break-up of her first marriage. Barrie both challenged and encouraged me as a young Christian and a young professional man, and as a husband, stepfather and father.

Peter Stevenson

For helping to keep me on the right path as a young man at university and for being an example and an inspiration (see chapter three).

Ian Higginbotham

My good friend and prayer partner for many years now, for being a tremendous source of strength to me as a confidant, a constant source of good ideas and encouragement, and especially for his consistently wise counsel.

Jim Martin and John Hicks

Two old friends, both of whom have been with me in various adventures and jolly japes over the years, usually revolving around sport of one kind or another. We have had a lot of fun together, and hopefully that will continue for many more years to come.

Dan Clement and Andy Tomlinson

My stepson and son respectively. I love you both, guys, and you have brought me great joy. You have also managed between you to cause me a fair amount of heartache over the last thirty years, but I still wouldn't be without either of you.

Christine Mary Tomlinson

My wife and my very best friend. How on earth you have managed to put up with me I can't imagine, but I'm just so very glad that you have.

Finally, I also owe a significant debt of gratitude to the people who have helped bring about the publication of these memoirs, and in particular:

Georgina Lamb

Regional Manager for RABI in the North West, she is responsible for managing events and developing sponsorship opportunities, and acts as the link between RABI and its volunteer county committees, and she does a great job in support of the charity's role in providing welfare and financial help to those in the farming community in need, hardship or distress. Thank you for being so enthusiastic about my crazy idea in the first place, and for sticking with me through the process.

Katharine Gardner

The wife of Andrew Gardner, the current senior pastor of Fulwood Free Methodist Church, and a very talented author and teacher of writing skills in her own right. Thank you for volunteering to read my original manuscript and then spending so much time and effort in doing a thorough and very professional job in editing my first attempt at this book. I am grateful to you for putting me right on quite a few things, and for helping me to keep relatively politically correct the final published version.

Dan Clement (again)

For your wonderful illustrations for this book. You have a very special talent, son.

Paul Stanier of Zaccmedia

For helping me get this book published.

What next? The exciting thing is that I really don't know what lies ahead for me. I'm certainly not done yet. I'm still blessed with good health and energy and I haven't lost my natural optimism and enthusiasm. My business partner John Woosnam once put a note on a greetings card which he had sent to me, saying that my optimism and enthusiasm would get me out of most of the scrapes they had got me into in the first place. They were wise words which have indeed been proved true, I'm pleased to say.

All I can say is that once I have retired I hope that I will be able to be of use to someone somewhere in terms of Christian service. I am open to suggestions.

I know this may sound like a cliché, but please bear with me on this one – when I applied to train as a solicitor the first stage of the process involved me attending a personal interview before a panel of three experienced solicitors appointed for the purpose by the Law Society. At the time, I was at Durham University so my interview took place in Newcastle. I suppose the main purpose was to establish whether or not I possessed the appropriate 'moral fibre' to be allowed to join the profession (although I can't help thinking that if it was, they have allowed a few bad ones to slip through the net!). All I can really remember of the interview is that I was asked why I wanted to become a solicitor, i.e. what was my main motivation for choosing this path. My response was that I wanted to do a job (actually I probably said 'wanted to join a profession') which would enable me to help people in some way.

Some might suggest that if that really was my motivation I should have become a doctor, or a social worker, or even a pastor, but that is honestly what has motivated me throughout my career. In fact, I believe firmly that that can apply to anyone, whatever might be their job or profession. I have had the privilege of guiding and helping many farming folk through some of the most difficult and stressful periods in their personal and business lives, and I just hope that I have done that in a positive and constructive way. It is for others to judge whether or not I have succeeded in my aim to help others through my career, but I do hope that I have managed it to some small degree, and that in due course I will be remembered as a man of integrity.

Lightning Source UK Ltd.
Milton Keynes UK
UKOW04f0329040314

227484UK00002B/77/P